Teacher for a Day - Early Childhood Edition

## Dear Fellow Teacher,

The purpose of this guide is to provide a comprehensive, user-friendly resource book. After the success of my first two books Teacher for a Day Primary and High School Editions I had lots of people request an Early Childhood Edition, so here it is!

I started my teaching career in Early Childhood and have over 8 years experience in a Childcare setting along with 8 years in a classroom. I was fortunate to work at an innovative and child-initiated community centre that gave me the skills to think on my feet to engage children in their learning by extending on their interests. This skill is invaluable to me and has helped me utilise those "teachable moments" in both a school and parental role. You will find lots of little activities and gems that you can easily implement to create more "teachable moments" in your room or home.

This book has all that you need compiled into one book. There are effective Behaviour Management Strategies, Daily Plan examples, an Organiser to record Professional Development, Work Expenses, Contact Details and more. The activities are split into age appropriate activities **0-2 years** and **3-6 years** and each section has a simplified explanation for why it is important for their learning. I'm less about being "Pinterest perfect" and more about the process and education behind the activity. The activities can be easily adjusted to suit the children's needs, some songs and activities in the 0-2 years section may be suitable for your 3 year olds, some 2 year olds will love an activity that the 5 year olds are doing. Nothing is written in stone so just use the age sections as a guide.

With over 200 engaging activities for children aged 0-6 years that need little preparation and no photocopying, I'm sure you will find plenty to educate and entertain your children in a meaningful way.

---

This guide is set into 16 different sections.

       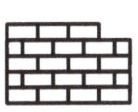

Tips | Organiser | Daily Plan and Notes | Routine and Transitions | Literacy | Numeracy | Art | Building

Science | Fine Motor Skills | Gross Motor Skills | Dramatic Play | Music | Games | Outdoor Activities | Sustainability

Each section is broken up into activities that are suited to either **0-2 YEARS** or **3-6 YEARS** or both.

The book also includes the following templates and items that may be useful.

### Resources included

- Daily Plan Template
- School Year Calendar
- Daily Plan suggestions and outline
- Professional Development recording sheet
- Financial Records sheet
- Engaging activities for 0-6 year olds

I hope this book makes your days easier and successful as well as sparking that joy of learning in your little ones.

Happy teaching!

*Kelly*

Copyright © 2017 by Kelly Quilter
ISBN 978-0-9954057-3-8

Contact: kelly@teacherforaday.com
Illustrations and Layout: msambayan.08@gmail.com
You can find more resources at www.teacherforaday.com

All rights reserved. This book or any portion thereof
may not be reproduced or used in any manner whatsoever
without the express written permission of the copy owner
except for the use of brief quotations in a book review.

# TEACHER FOR A DAY

The All - in - One Resource for Engaging Children and Succeeding as an Early Childhood Educator

## Early Childhood Edition

by Kelly Quilter

Illustrations by Emmanuel Sambayan

For my siblings,
**Daniel and Jodie**
For all the awesome memories
we created throughout our
childhood.

# CONTENTS

## Tips

| | |
|---|---|
| 18 | Things to Remember |
| 19 | 13 Tips to Make Your Day Run Smoothly |
| 20 | Open Ended Questioning and Activities |
| 21 | Behaviour Management Tips |
| 22 | Behaviour Management Strategies |
| 24 | What Parents Want... |
| 26 | Resource Suggestions |
| 32 | Developmental Red Flags |
| 33 | Independent Skills |

## Organiser

| | |
|---|---|
| 36 | Important Contact Details |
| 38 | School Year Calendar |
| 42 | Work Expenses |
| 44 | Professional Development Records |
| 46 | Important Dates |
| 47 | School Terms and Holiday Dates |

## Daily Plan and Notes

| | |
|---|---|
| 50 | Learning Area Keys |
| 51 | Daily Plan Template |
| 52 | Babies Room (0-2 years) |
| 53 | Toddlers (2-3 years) |
| 54 | Kindy (3-4 years) |
| 55 | Pre School (4-6 years) |
| 56 | Daily Outdoor Setup |
| 58 | Critical Reflections |

## Routine and Transitions

**64  Daily Routine Songs**
  Morning Songs
   Make a Circle
   Days of the Week
   Good Morning to You
   Tell Me What Your Name Is
   Bee Bee Bumble Bee
   Hey Good Morning
   Where is _____?

**65  Goodbye Songs**
   Where are the Children?
   It's Time to End the Day
   This is the Way We Say Goodbye

# Table of Contents

## Routine and Transitions

**65** **Transition**
  Transition Games
   *Actions*
   *Go if You're...*
   *If Your Name Is...*
**66** *I Spy*
  *Partners*
  *Identify It*
  *Find your Name*
  *Wibbly Wobbly*
  *Spelling Names*

**67** **Transition Songs**
  *Five Currant Buns*
  *Five Cheeky Monkeys Swinging in the Tree*
  *Five Cheeky Monkeys Jumping on the Bed*
  *One Grey Elephant*
  *Ten in the Bed*
  *Five Fat Sausages*
  *If You're Wearing*
  *Five Little Duck*
  *Three Jellyfish*

**68** **Packing Away Ideas**
  *Cues*
  *Cleaning Time*
  *A Clean Race*
  *Tidy Tongs*
  *Magic Item*
  *Model*
  *Cleaning Freeze*
**69** *Magical Roleplay*
  *Simon Says*
  *Star Cleaners*
  *Beat the Buzzer*

**69** Pack Away Songs
  *The More We Help Together*
  *Time to Clean Up*
  *Pack Away*
  *This is the Way We Pack Away*
  *It's Time to Pack Away*
  *Pick it Up and Pack It Up*

## Literacy

**74** **Babies & Toddlers**
  **Pre Literacy Skills**

**74** **3-6 Years**
  **Pre Literacy Skills**
   *Rhyming Books*
   *Alphabet Search*
   *Alphabet Detective*
**75** *Collage a List*
  *Lists*
  *Repetitive Books*
  *Open-Ended Questioning*

**76** **Reading**
  Reading Strategies
  Questioning
   *Literal*
   *Inferential*
   *Evaluative*

**77** **0-2 years**
   *Touchy-Feely Pre-Reading*
   *Noisy Stories*
   *Familiar Faces*
   *Story Telling*
   *Interesting Read*

**78** **2-4 years**
  *Story Telling*
  *Nursery Rhymes*
  *ABC*
  *Predict It*
  *Name Tags*

**79** **4-6 years**
  *Tons of Texts*
  *Look it up*
  *Read for Pleasure*
  *Story Sequencing*
**80** *Rhyming Basket*
  *Rhyme It*
  *Find the Rhyme*
**81** *Syllable Clap*
  *Super Pointer*

**82** **Letter Work**
  Letter sounds

**82** **3-6 years**
  *Rhyme It*
  *CVC Words*
  *Creative Letters*
  *Letter Find*

# Table of Contents

## Literacy

**83** 3-6 years
 Sound Sort
 Missing Sounds
 Alphabet Hunt
 One Day I Went Walking...
**84** Eye Spy
 ABC Jump
 Alphabet Card Games
 Letter Case Matching
 Onset and Rime

**85** **Writing**
 0-2 years
 Cotton Tip Painting
 Drawing in Sand
 Drawing

**86** **Pre- Writing Line Development**
 3 years
 4 years
 5 years
**87** Pencil Grasps
 Highlighter Tracing
 Dot to Dot
 Tally Marks
 Cotton Tip Painting
 Laminated Tracing
 Paper Tracing
**88** 3-6 years
 Draw a Monster/Clown

**90** **Speaking and Listening**
 0-2 years
 Picture Cues
**91** Action Songs
 Following Instructions
 Peek - a - boo

**92** 3-6 years
 Sound Patterns
 Follow the Leader
 Do What I Say, Not What I Do
**93** Simon Says
 Tounge Twisters
 Opposites
**94** Follow Directions
 Draw Directions
 Find the Opposites
 Be the Teacher

**95** **Memory and Recall**
 0-2 years
 Where Is?
 Routine
 Packing Away
 Silly Dressing
 Name It
 Songs
 What Sound?
 3-6 years
**96** Categorise It
 Learn a Poem or Song
 Who's Missing?
 Pick the Missing Object
 Story Recall
 Memory Match
**97** Morning Routine
 I Went to the Shop
 Object Hunt

## Numeracy

**102** Maths for 0-2 years
 Fill Them Up
 Size Them Up
 Patterns in the World
 Colour Sorting
 Shapes
 Block Tower Patterns
 Shapes
 Nesting Game

**103** Counting in their world
 Puzzles
 Tall Towers
 Object Sorting
 Matchy Matchy
 AB Patterning

## Numeracy

**104** Maths for 3-6 years
  **Counting**
  *Dice Stamping*
  *Tallying*
**105** *Counting One-to-One*
  *Subitizing*
  *Dice Dots*
**106** **Shapes**
  *Shape Pictures*
  *Trace a Shape*
  *Shape Sorting*
  *Shapes in Our World*
**107** **Patterns**
  *Growing Patterns*
  *Pattern People*
  *Repeated Patterns*
  *Movement Patterns*
  *Pattern Jewellery*
**108** *Missing Patterns*
  *Symmetry*
  *Symmetry Art*
**109** **Positional and Directional Language**
  *Directional words*
  *Directional Maze*
**110** *Following Directions*
  *Positional numbers*

**110** **Matching and Sorting**
  *Objects to Sort*
**111** *Graphing*
**112** **Measurement**
  3-6 years
  *Line Them Up*
  *Same Same or Different*
  *Get in Order*
  *Family Portrait*
  *Towers*
**113** *Measure Me*
  *How Long Is Your Name?*
**114** *Balancing Act*
  *Marble Capacity*
  *Block Area*
  *Volume*
  *Choose your Measurements*
**115** **Time**
  *Days of the Week*
  *Months*
  *Seasons*
  *Dress for the Season*
  *Season Themes*

## Art

**120** Different Types of Art Supplies to Use
**121** Things to Use Instead of Paper
**122** Alternative Painting ideas without a paintbrush
  *Blocks*
  *Rubber Gloves*
  *Bubbles*
  *Pegs*
**123** *Toothpicks*
  *Utensils*
  *Fishing Rod Painting*
  *Candles*
**124** *Marbles*
  *Cars*
  *Food*
  *Spray Bottles*
**125** *Tools*
  *Paint Pens*
  *Feathers*
  *Fingers, Toes, or Body*
  *Ice Cube Painting*
  *Fly Swatter*
**126** *Nature Art*
**128** **Drawing**
  *Shadow Drawing*
  *Squiggles*
  *Directed Drawing*
**129** *Colour Tracing*
  *Tracing Templates*
  *Paper Roll Scribblers*

Teacher for a Day

## TABLE OF CONTENTS

### Building

- 134 Alphabet Blocks
- Velcro Blocks
- Block Maze
- 135 Stacking Objects
- Block Recreation
- Train tracks
- Duplo or Lego
- 135 Wooden Blocks
- 136 Race Tracks
- Train Tracks
- Foamy Foam Blocks
- 137 Building a River
- Stick Structures

### Science

- 142 Cornflour Slime
- Sink and Float
- 143 Vinegar Volcano
- Self-inflating Balloon
- 144 Flying Paper Planes
- Scented Painting
- 145 Colourful Absorption
- Growing Seedlings
- 146 Musical Straw
- Floating Egg
- 147 Static Electricity
- Tie-dye Surface Tension

### Fine Motor Skills

- 152 **0-2 years**
- Droppers
- Shake It
- Play Dough
- Finger Plays and Rhymes
- Texture Play
- Nature Play
- Scrunching Paper
- Cars
- Drawing
- 153 Pom Pom Push
- Feely Board or Boxes
- Cooking
- Stick Threading
- 154 **3-6 years**
- Feely Bags
- Dress Ups
- Grab It
- 154 Box Collage
- Magnets
- Carpentry
- Lego
- Messy Play
- Tracing
- Washing Babies
- Tactile Picture
- Play Dough
- 155 Threading
- Drawing
- Paper Boll Toss
- Cutting
- 156 **Play Dough**
- Play Dough Recipe
- Things to put the play dough on
- 157 Things to add with play dough
- Tools to use with play dough

### Gross Motor Skills

- 162 Skills to Practise
- 163 Obstacle Course
- Skipping Rope
- 164 Yoga
- 164 Climbing
- Ball Skills
- 165 Hop, Skip and Jump Hopstoch
- Hoops

## Table of Contents

## Dramatic Play

170 Clusters
Bean Game
171 Minute Mime
Animal Walk
Intro and Applause
172 Dress Ups
Puppets
Fairy Tale Plays

172 Play Shops
Doctors
173 Restaurant
Offices
Beauty Salon
Post Office
Archaeologist
Pets

## Music

178 **0-2 years**
Musical Freeze
Five Little Ducks
Rain Rain Go Away
Head, Shoulders, Knees and Toes
Five Little Monkeys
179 Five Little Speckled Frogs
Where is Thumbkin?
Old MacDonald Had a Farm
One Two Buckle My Shoe
180 Miss Polly Had a Dolly
If You're Happy And You Know It
Little Peter Rabbit
This Little Piggy
Rock-a-Bye Baby
181 The Wheels on The Bus
One Two Three Four Five
Teddy Bear, Teddy Bear
Row Row Row Your Boat
Ring-a-rosie
See Saw Margery Daw
Round and Round The Garden
Twinkle Twinkle Little Star
Ten Little Fingers
I Hear Thunder

182 **3-6 years**
Musical Chairs
Found Sound
Storm Musical
Doggy, Doggy Where's Your Bone?
183 Who stole the Cookie from the Cookie Jar?
Sound Patterns
Soft and Loud

184 **Action songs**
Music Man
Bingo
I'm Taking Home my Baby Bumble Bee

184 Wind The Bobbin Up
Hokey Pokey
Sleeping Bunnies
185 Dingle Dangle Scarecrow
The Farmer in The Dell
Brush Your Teeth
A Sailor Went To Sea
I'm a Peanut
186 This Old Man
187 Johnny Works with One Hammer
Ten Green Bottles
188 Ten Little Indians
Here is the Beehive
One Little Finger
Ants Go Marching

189 **Nursery Rhymes**
Mary Had a Little Lamb
Baa Baa Black Sheep
I'm a Little Teapot
Little Bo Beep
Little Miss Muffet
Little Jack Horner
190 Humpty Dumpty
Hey Diddle Diddle
It's Raining, It's Pouring
Pat-a-Cake
The Grand Old Duke of York
Three Blind Mice
191 Jack and Jill
Mary Mary Quite Contrary
Polly Put The Kettle On
Sing a Song of Sixpence
There Was a Crooked Man
Incy Wincy Spider
Old Mother Hubbard
Hot Cross Buns
Hickory Dickory Dock

# TABLE OF CONTENTS

## Games

**196** **1-3 years**
*Duck, Duck, Goose*
*Musical Statues*
*Stop! Go! Fast! Slow!*

**197** **3-6 years**
*Hot and Cold*
*What's the Time Mr. Wolf?*
*Balloon Up*
**198** *Pizza Massage*
*Corners*
*Scissors, Paper, Rock*
**199** *Mr. Squiggle*
*Poison Letter*

## Outdoor Activities

**204** **Outdoor Activity Setup**
*Sandpit*
**205** *Water Play*
**206** *Obstacle Course*
*Sport Time*
*Bikes, Cars and Scooters*
*Fairy Garden*
*Teddy Bears Picnic*
**207** *Bring Inside, Outside*
*Cubbyhouse*
*Blocks*
*Art and Craft*

**208** **Parachute Games**
*Waves*
*Dome*
*Popcorn*
*Poisonous Snake*
**209** *Parachute Tiggy*
*Rolling Ball*
*Name Change*
*Bouncy Balls*

## Sustainability

**214** Be Water Wise

**215** **Waste Warriors**
*Litterbug*
*Reduce*
**216** *Reuse*
*Recycle*
**217** *Power Saver*
*Walk, Don't Drive*

"Children must be taught how to think,
not what to think."

**Margaret Mead**

# Tips

Teacher for a Day

# THINGS TO REMEMBER

All children, especially young children have their own distinct personalities and needs. What works for one child might not work for the next.

Remember to practise patience and compassion towards the children who are in your care.

Be playful, fun and enthusiastic.

Be positive and use encouraging language to help instil confidence in their abilities.

Get to know the children. Learn their likes, dislikes, their interests and their skills

Spend time just talking to them and you will watch them grow and blossom before your very eyes.

*Early Childhood Edition*

# 13 TIPS TO MAKE YOUR DAY RUN SMOOTHLY

1. Arrive early to prepare activities. Art activities can be particularly fiddly so get these ready ahead of time.

2. Be approachable and address parents and children on arrival. Ask the parents if there is anything you need to know, last bottle, sleep times etc.

3. Be mindful of when a parent needs your assistance when trying to leave their child. Ask the parent directly to let them know when they need you to take their child.

4. Drop offs can be horrible for both children and parents so make sure you have a distraction for the child if they are upset. Reassure the parents that they will be fine and tell the parents they are welcome to call at anytime to check on their child.

5. Part of your role is to help children learn how to play, interact and make friends. It doesn't come as naturally to some so encourage role play, games and friendships. The younger children prefer to play alongside each other but some older children need more encouragement so pair up children you think would get along.

6. Make learning meaningful but fun. Children have their whole lives to be drilled with skills. These years are the times to encourage curiosity to foster a love for learning early on. If you get resistance, don't sweat it, it will happen when they are ready.

7. Extending on their interests is the easiest way to plan your activities whilst giving the students ownership and engagement as it was from their initiative.

8. Model everything. Be VERY explicit in your explanations. Show them exactly how the activity is done. Give them examples of ideas or answers you are looking for. They are learning expectations of a classroom from how to sit nicely on the mat to how to take turns with peers.

9. You will learn amazing things when you take the time to listen to the children. Be conscious to take time to engage with every child throughout the day.

10. Be consistent with your expectations and follow through, however children at this age need love and warmth so be sure to keep a healthy balance.

11. Be enthusiastic about EVERYTHING. This will get them more excited and involved in what they are doing. Be childish, be silly, be fun. Pretend like you're on Sesame Street!

12. Make it a competition. "I wonder if the boys can be the quietest walking out to lunch? Now girls, can you beat them?" "Who here can sit the straightest on the carpet?" "I want to see who can be the quietest to go choose an activity." It's amazing how quickly others will follow suit in order to "win" or gain positive attention.

13. Positive reinforcement is key with this age group. Comments like "*I love the way you are sitting nicely on the mat,*" "*I'm proud of you for sharing with your friend,*" or "*Great job packing away.*" Children this age (generally) love to please so praise will always reinforce and encourage more positive behavior. Promote a growth mindset by praising effort and the process rather than the person and qualities such as intelligence or talent. Say things like "Great work, you must have tried really hard."

Teacher for a Day

# OPEN ENDED QUESTIONING AND ACTIVITIES

**Open ended questioning**

There are two types of questioning, open and closed. Closed questions are your typical who, what, where and when questions that require one single, correct answer. Open ended questions require a more critical or creative answer, encouraging more of a discussion. These are usually prompted by asking how and why and it is this style of questioning that encourages critical thinking.

This can be done simply by asking the children before you start reading a book what they think it might be about by using just the title and illustrations. These predictions allow them to think critically and analytically before you've even started reading.

Open ended questions also help develop their language and vocabulary skills as it requires them to give more than a one word answer. Closed questions require them to answer based on what they think should be the right answer, open ended questions allow them to answer more freely, using their own ideas, thoughts and judgements. It helps create group discussions with others, teaching turn taking, patience and how to work together as they learn about other's point of view, ideas or opinions.

**Some examples of Open Ended Questions**

What do you think might happen next?
Can you describe what happened?
Could you figure out a different way to do that?
Do you have any other ideas?
How could we work this out?
How are they alike/different?
How did you feel?
How did you know that?
Tell me how you worked that out together?
Tell me about what you made/created/built?
Tell me about what you did?
Tell me about what you saw?
What did you like best about it?
What did you notice about?
What problems did you come across?
What would you do differently next time?
What made you choose _____ over _____?

**Extension on these questions-**
- Paraphrase what they have told you. Repeat the information by adding in different vocabulary and information.

- Encourage further explanation by getting them to show you, draw or write for you what they are thinking.

**Avoid questions that only require a YES, NO, MAYBE or one word answer.**

# BEHAVIOUR MANAGEMENT TIPS

- Young children have varying cognitive abilities and needs that you need to take into consideration. Treat each child equally but be aware of their individual needs too.

- Redirection is a vital strategy to use. Move a child away from a situation they shouldn't be in or suggest a different activity or area to them if trouble is arising.

- Try not to resort to yelling. A calm, quiet voice or a stern look can be just as effective when trying to get your point across.

- If an activity isn't working, don't keep persevering with it. Choose an activity you know will engage them. If the children are engaged they will be less likely to get up to mischief!

- Be mindful to use positive words rather than negative words. Cut down on 'no's' and 'stops' and swap them with the behaviour you want them to do as they will often only hear the action you are saying in the phrase. For instance instead of:

    - "Stop running inside," say "Walking feet inside."
    - "No climbing" say "Feet on the floor."
    - "No hitting" say "We keep our hands to ourselves"
    - "No spitting," say "Yucky germs will spread if we do that."

You will never rid your vocabulary of 'no's' and 'stops' but with practise you will get better at using more positive language to redirect and teach good behaviour in these little humans.

- Make sure that the students are being challenged physically and mentally through varying activities. Young children have a lot of energy to burn and a thirst for knowledge so use this to your advantage to avoid behavioural issues.

- Take a difficult child aside, get down on their level and speak to them one on one away from the class. This way they cannot get the attention from peers that they usually crave. Explain that you are unhappy with their behaviour and suggest that they change it now or there will be further consequences.

- If any behaviour gets out of hand or dangerous, firstly make sure the other children are safe then call on your Director if you don't feel able to deal with it.

- Use a bell or song to signal pack away times so the children instantly know the cues.

- Bored children will tend to find trouble or resort to play fighting and rough housing with others.

- An enthusiastic teacher that shows warmth, interest and engages meaningfully with the children will build rapport quickly which is key when gaining the trust of young children.

- Routine is very important, so set up and follow a general routine so that children can learn the classroom expectations and anticipate the schedule.

- Be very explicit in your directions. Demonstrate exactly what your expectations are to help them learn and understand how to behave appropriately.

# BEHAVIOUR MANAGEMENT STRATEGIES

Outline your expectations for their behaviour and what the disciplinary actions will be.

### Calls to Attention

Teach the children little call and responses to get their attention. You say the first part and they answer with the second.

1, 2, 3. Eyes on me…1,2. Eyes on you.
Hands on top… Everybody stop!
Macaroni and Cheese…Yes please!
Shark bait…Hoo ha ha!
To infinity… And beyond!
Holy moly… Guacamole!
Waterfall…Shhhh!
Flat tire… Shhh!
Can I get a… Whoop! Whoop!
Stop!...Collaborate and listen!
All set?... You bet!
Ready to rock… Ready to roll!
Zip it, lock it…Put it in your pocket.

### Teacher Says

Teacher says "Freeze! Put your hands on your heads. Put your hands on your knees, Toes, mouth etc. until you have all the children's attention.

If you are sitting on the carpet you can do repeated patterns silently until all students catch on. Touch head, ears, head, ears. Then nose, shoulders, nose, shoulders etc.

Early Childhood Edition

### Musical attention

Ringing a bell, a shaker, tambourine or other musical instrument is the perfect way to get the classes attention for transitions. Even a particular song being played can be a fun signal to get them to stop what they are doing and refocus.

### Positive Rewards

Stickers, Stamps and Certificates are the perfect, inexpensive way to reinforce positive behaviour. It could be a stamp for the children packing away the best, a sticker for those showing good listening or a certificate for children showing kind behaviour. Giving more attention to positive behaviours will encourage them to act in this manner more frequently.

### Perform a Trick

Tell them if they do fantastic listening then you will do something special for them at the end such as a cartwheel, handstand, push-ups or any other fun skill you have. They will do anything to see you being silly and you will always be fondly remembered for any wacky things you do.

### Star of the Day

You could choose a person to be the Star of the Day. That child can be a special helper or could receive a certificate or special toy to take home and return next time they attend.

**TIPS**

Teacher for a Day

# WHAT PARENTS WANT...

Ultimately our job is to make sure the children are safe and happy and parents are the ones to decide whether you adequately meet their child's needs. Parents want the very best for their child and some aren't afraid to let you know. These Do's and Don'ts will ensure parents are happy so in turn making your boss happy. Win-win!

- Be smiley and happy. A warm smile goes a long way.

- Record any incidents that would need to be recorded.

- Call parents if it is something they should be notified of. A scraped knee, probably not, a significant bump to the head, definitely.

- Remember to pass on any messages to staff when you finish your shift

- Act professionally at all times.

- Make sure the room is clean and tidy. "If you have time to lean, you have time to clean." Young children aren't as aware or capable of keeping their germs to themselves so in order to avoid illnesses spreading, it is important to keep the place clean.

- Offer a wide variety of activities. The children need to be exposed to many experiences to develop their skills. Let your imagination run wild and have fun with the children.

- Talk, interact and play with the children. Learn their likes and dislikes, their strengths and weaknesses and then extend and work on those things.

Early Childhood Edition

- Don't spend all day talking to staff. All too often staff fall into the trap of workplace gossip and forget what they are really there for, the children. Save the chat for lunch breaks.

- Don't disclose inappropriate information about your personal life or other children to parents.

- Don't worry if the children's work isn't "Pintrest-worthy." It's about the learning process, not the end product.

- Don't leave the room layout the same for too long. The children love exploring new things and something as simple as the home corner being moved can bring new interest and life to the area.

- Don't send a child home in wet or soiled clothing and grubby faces. They trust you to take care of the child as if they were your own so don't abuse that trust.

- Don't say negative things constantly to parents that have "that" child. Try to find the small positives to help celebrate their child's progress.

Teacher for a Day

# RESOURCE SUGGESTIONS
## Suggested books with activities

### 0-3 years — Spot Series by Eric Hill

These books are always a hit, particularly with the younger children. Extend language and promote reading skills by asking questions throughout the book such as-

- What do you think is under the flap?
- What sound does that animal make?
- What is this? (Pointing to an object)
- Where is the _____?
- What colour is the _____?

### 3-6 years — The Very Cranky Bear Series by Nick Bland

These books are a fun selection. Great for practising rhyme and rhythm. They include- The Very Cranky Bear, The Very Hungry Bear, The Very Noisy Bear, The Very Brave Bear, The Very Itchy Bear.

|  | Cranky | Hungry | Noisy | Brave | Itchy |
|---|---|---|---|---|---|
| DISCUSSION | **Emotions** What makes you cranky? Do a cranky face. What helps you turn that cranky mood around? Will what make you happy be what makes someone else happy? Why do you think the sheep was the only one to offer the right solution? (Because she listened!) | **Sustainability** Why was the polar bear so fussy with where he could stay? (need somewhere cool, icy and large). Discuss the issues of global warming and how pollution is causing the icebergs to melt. What animals would be affected? What would happen to those animals if all the icebergs melted? | **Strengths** Why did the bear try so many instruments? Was he good at all the instruments? Why is it a good thing to keep trying different things? Is there something you weren't very good at but got better at with practise? | **Bravery** What are you scared of? Show me with your body how to be scared? What does it mean to be brave? Show me with your body how to be brave. When was a time that you overcame your fear and were brave? | **Friendship** Did Bear like the flea at the start? Why not? What happened by the end of the book? Have you felt lonely like Bear in the story? How does being lonely make you feel? How can we make others not feel lonely? |
| ACTIVITIES | **Do a Good Deed** Set a challenge for the children to do something kind for someone else. Give examples of ways they can do this and get them to report back at group time. **Paint a Picture** Paint the bear with a mane, stripes and antlers. **Craft** Create a mane out of crepe paper, stripes out of electrical tape and antlers using sticks to dress up a teddy bear. | **Who Eats What?** Get children to match an animal to a food. This could be a drawing on the board or matching cut-out pictures on the floor. **Meat, Plant or Both?** Discuss the meaning of the words "herbivore, omnivore and carnivore" and try to decide which animal fits in which category. You could research on the internet to help you work it out. | **Air Instruments** Discuss the instruments in the book and get them to pretend to play them. Ask them if they know any other instruments and how they are played. **Music Time** Bring out real instruments and practise the difference between playing them properly and not so appropriately. **Loud vs Soft** Practise making noise ranging from loud to silent using the teacher's cues. This could be with instruments or using your body. | **I Can Do It Better!** What were Boris and Bear trying to do the whole time? (outdo each other). Do you ever try to do something better than someone else? Is that ok? (yes as long as you are kind about it and not doing it just to show off). Discuss how people have different things they are good at. Share one thing you think you are good at to the group. **Draw a Picture** Draw a picture of when you were brave like Boris and the Bear. | **Rhyme Time** Discuss the rhyming words in the book and get the children to come up with new rhyming words. They can be real or nonsense but try to get them to decide which one they are. **What's Itchy?** Show me what it's like to be itchy? (Get them scratching!) What things can make you itch? (mosquito, sandflies, fleas, nits, rash, chickenpox, allergies). Get them to act out the itches of different things e.g. Slapping mosquitos, scratching a nit filled head. |

Early Childhood Edition

## The Gruffalo by Julia Donaldson

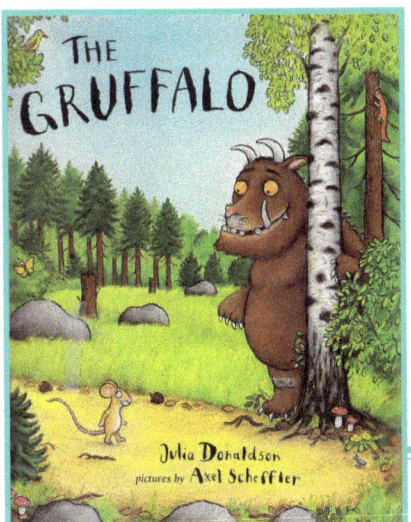

Ask questions as you are reading the text such as-

Looking at the cover, where is the story set?
What do you think a Gruffalo is? Is it real?
What other animals might you find in the woods?
Why would the fox/owl/snake want to invite a mouse to tea?
Why would the mouse say "No."?
Would you like to eat Roasted Fox, Owl Ice cream, Scrambled Snake or Gruffalo Crumble?
Why would the Mouse's tummy rumble?
Has your tummy rumbled before?

### Rhyme Time
Get them to predict the rhyming words as you read the text. Get children to come up with different rhyming words.

### Tricky words
Check for understanding of tricky words such as tusks, sped, knobbly knees, turned-out toes, poisonous wart, feast, logpile house, purple prickles, hid, slid, creature, oh crumbs, astounding, fled.

### Emotions
Discuss the emotions of the characters in the book. How do their expressions change? How are they feeling? Why would they feel like that?

## Press Here and Mix it Up! by Herve Tullet

Press Here is a funny, interactive book that younger students love. Reading for enjoyment at it's best.

- Get students to create their own page with dots using paint.
- Create patterns using coloured sticker dots. Try 2 then 3 colour combinations then try large and small dot patterns. They can draw or paint if no stickers are available.

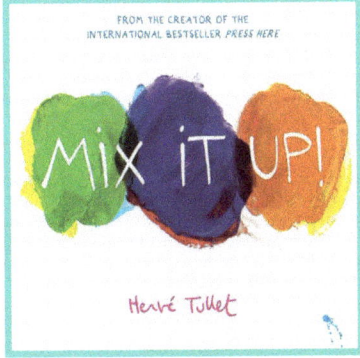

Mix it Up is an interactive book about colours. Great to lead into an art activity to explore colour mixing or the colour wheel.

- Draw around your hand on white paper then add colour splotches with paint around to look like the page of the book.

- Explore mixing colours with paint by creating folded colour splotches like they do in the book to mix the colours up and see what they change to.

- Discuss how primary colours mix up to create secondary colours. Show them the colour wheel and get them to create their own.

TIPS

Teacher for a Day

### This is a ball by Beck and Matt Stanton

This hilarious book drives kids nuts as they try to correct you.

**Questions**
How do you know it is not a ball? (balls don't have edges or corners)

What would a blue tomato taste like?

**Language of Chance**
Discuss the language of chance. To what degree of certainty do the words in the text mean by "definitely" (certain) and "no way" (impossible)?

Set up two sides that are "Definitely or Certain" and "No way or Impossible" then give other scenarios for them to rank on the scale such as-

*It will be Monday tomorrow.
A dragon will appear in the room.
You will have dinner tonight.
A fish will swim in the sea.
It's your birthday tomorrow.
You will meet a fairy tonight.*

### Fat Rabbit Series by Wayne Patterson

A set of four fabulous books that the kids love. They feature engaging pictures, educational and social learning and lots of repetition allowing children to participate in the story. Plus, proceeds go to finding a cure for Motor Neurone Disease.

| Fat Rabbit | Fat Rabbit Counts | Fat Rabbit's Burp | Fat Rabbit and the Cheeky Coconuts |
|---|---|---|---|
| Practise question and response. "Do you like _____?" "Yes, I like _____." | Practise counting skills from 1 to 10. Try counting backwards from 10 to 1. | Identify differences in the burps- smell, shape and colour. | Ask children how they would feel if this happened to them. What would they do? Is there something you do sometimes that might annoy others? |
| Come up with new activities that Fat Rabbit might like to do. | One-to-one correspondence- pointing to the objects as you count. | Discuss the describing words- beautiful, happy, sad, confused, round, fat etc. | How was the problem solved? Recall a time that you solved a problem with friends. |
| Discuss or draw a picture of something you like to do. | Practise identifying and writing numbers. | Practise positional words- up, down, under, over etc. | Discuss respect for others, using manners and how we can stand up for ourselves like Fat Rabbit did. |
| Role play activities in the book. | Students draw objects in the book with the corresponding number. | Recall- Where did Fat Rabbit look first? Who did he ask? | Sequence the events of the story. |
| Charades- Act out something Fat Rabbit likes to do and children need to guess. | Hop, skip and bounce around the room getting children to count different objects as you pass them. | Describe or draw the characters. | Directed drawing of Fat Rabbit or one of the other characters. |
| Survey the class to find the three most popular Fat Rabbit activities. You could then graph the results. | Build 3 sandcastles in the sandpit like in the story. | Who else could he ask? What would their burp be like? Describe the new character and their burp. | Design a coconut character with its own personality. |
| Grow carrot tops in a dish of water. | Draw a map of Carrot Top Island with some of the objects from the book on it. | Discuss how the characters use their manners and how and when the children use theirs. | |
| Make Fat Rabbit masks out of paper plates. | | | |

Early Childhood Edition

## Do Not Open This Book by Andy Lee

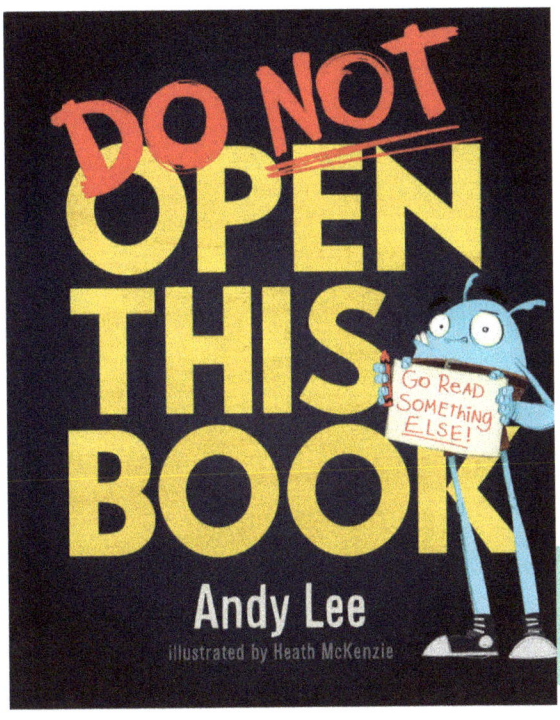

A fun book that has the students calling out in anticipation.

- Get students to come up with a new ending as to what will happen if they get to the last page. Could it be an alien instead of a witch? What else could he turn into?

- Ask students why we kept wanting to turn the page even though we were told not to? Is there any situation they have been in that they have been told not to do something but did it anyway?

Write it down or tell of a situation you were really tempted to do something you were told not to do.

## The Book with No Pictures by B.J. Novak

The class will be shouting at you to see the next page. This book is always a hit but is recommended from 3+ age groups.

- Discuss how they felt about a book with no pictures at the start. Did they change their mind by the end?

- Get the children to make up their own nonsense words, define them and use them in a sentence.

*E.g. Frimp means to walk sideways really fast.*

Help them to make up a sentence to use their new made up word.

*I had to frimp through the bushes to get away from the jaguar.*

- Get the children to draw illustrations for the book.

TIPS

## Suggested websites for interactive resources

If you have access to the Internet use an interactive game or video to help engage the students on the topic they are learning.

### Websites

**ABCYa** | www.abcya.com
Free website with interactive games in Literacy, Numeracy, Holidays, Strategy and Skills.

**Brainzy** | www.education.com/games
Fun interactive literacy and numeracy games

**Funbrain** | www.funbrain.com
Stories, educational games and more on this free, fun website.

**GoNoodle** | www.gonoodle.com
Integrating mindfulness and movement in a fun way.

**Nat Geo Kids** | www.natgeokids.com/au/
Answer all their questions about animals and the world by researching through this child-friendly site.

**PBS Kids** | www.pbskids.org
Interactive games incorporating familiar T.V. shows

**Starfall ABC** | www.starfall.com
A reading website and app that starts with alphabet skills and assists them all the way to reading independently.

**Wonderopolis** | www.wonderopolis.org
For those inquisitive minds and to answer the million and one "why" questions!

**YouTube** | www.youtube.com
This is a great resource to watch videos on any topic you can imagine. Working on phonics? There will be some great sing-a-longs you could find. A child is wondering what turtles eat? You can show them footage of sea turtles eating in the wild.

## Apps

There are many great apps out there and for this age group Duck Duck Moose, 22 Learn and Toca Boca have lots of great ones. Here are just a few fun and education apps suitable for the Early Years.

### Literacy

**ABC Wildlife**
Learning letters and spelling for the animal lovers.

**Intro to Letters by Montessorium**
This simplistic design helps children recognise, pronounce and write letters.

**Phonics Fun on Farm by 22Learn**
Working on sounds and reading skills.

**Word Wagon by Duck Duck Moose**
App for interactive learning of letters, words and phonics.

### Maths

**Bugs and Numbers**
An adaptive game developing basic number skills in an engaging app the kids will love.

**Moose Math by Duck Duck Moose**
Numeracy app that works on number sense, shapes, addition, subtraction and skip counting.

**Park Math by Duck Duck Moose**
Maths app to develop skills in counting, addition, subtraction, sorting and patterns.

**Pre-K Basic Skills by 22Learn**
This app covers lots of basics- matching, colours, shapes, letters, numbers, patterns, puzzles, sizes, shadows, same and different and things that go together.

### Other Skills

**Touch and Learn- Emotions**
An app for self-awareness, empathy and identification of emotions.

**Dexteria**
an app to strengthen writing muscles through interactive play.

**Thinking Time Pro**
Cognitive Skills for Early Learning- Following directions, logic, memory and attention.

**Smiling Minds**
App with modern, guided meditation.

# Developmental Red Flags

As Educators it is important that we are observing children and ensuring they are meeting their milestones. Often parents rely on our opinions as they aren't sure what is regarded as 'normal' or 'abnormal' development. Early intervention is key so advise your Senior Staff if you notice a child not meeting their normal milestones.

**Here are some Red Flags to look out for-**

| | 6 months | 9 months | 12 months | 18 months | 2 years | 3 years | 4 years | 5 years | Red Flags at any stage |
|---|---|---|---|---|---|---|---|---|---|
| **Social/Emotional** | Does not smile or squeal in response to people | Not sharing enjoyment with others using eye contact or facial expression | Does not notice someone new; Does not play early turn taking games (e.g. peekaboo, rolling a ball) | Lacks interest in playing and interacting with others | When playing with toys tends to bang, drop, or throw them rather than use them for their purpose (e.g. cuddle doll, build blocks) | No interest in pretend play or other children; Difficulties in noticing and understanding feelings in themselves and others (e.g. happy, sad) | Unwilling / unable to play cooperatively | Play is different than their friends | Not achieving indicated developmental milestones; Strong parent concerns; Significant loss of skills; Lack of response to sound or visual stimuli; Poor interaction with adults or other children; Difference between right and left sides of body in strength, movement or tone; Loose and floppy movements (low tone) or stiff and tense (high tone) |
| **Communication** | Not starting to babble (e.g adah; oogoo) | No gestures (e.g. pointing, showing, waving); Not using 2 part babble (e.g. gaga, arma) | No babbled phrases that sound like talking; No response to familiar words | No clear words; Cannot understand short requests e.g. 'Where is the ball?' | Does not have at least 50 words; Not putting words together e.g. 'push car'; Most of what is said is not easily understood | Speech difficult to understand; Not using simple sentences e.g. big car go | Speech difficult to understand; Unable to follow directions with 2 steps | Difficulty telling a parent what is wrong; Cannot answer questions in a simple conversation | |
| **Fine Motor and Cognition** | Not reaching for and holding (grasping) toys; Hands frequently clenched | Unable to hold and/or release toys; Cannot move toy from one hand to another | Majority of nutrition still liquid/puree; Cannot chew solid food; Unable to pick up small items using index finger and thumb | Not holding or scribbling with a crayon; Does not attempt to tower blocks | No interest in self care skills e.g. feeding, dressing | Difficulty helping with self care skills (e.g. feeding, dressing); Difficulty manipulating small objects e.g. threading beads | Not toilet trained by day; Unable to draw lines and circles | Concerns from teacher about school readiness; Not independent with eating and dressing; Cannot draw simple pictures (e.g. stick person) | |
| **Gross Motor** | Not rolling; Not holding head and shoulders up when on tummy | Not sitting without support; Not moving e.g. creeping or crawling motion; Does not take weight well on legs when held by an adult | Not crawling or bottom shuffling; Not pulling to stand; Not standing holding on to furniture | Not attempting to walk without support; Not standing alone | Unable to run; Unable to use stairs holding on; Unable to throw a ball | Not running well; Cannot walk up and down stairs; Cannot kick or throw a ball; Cannot jump with 2 feet together | Cannot pedal a tricycle; Cannot catch, throw or kick a ball; Cannot balance well standing on one leg | Awkward when walking, running, climbing and using stairs; Ball skills are very different to their peers; Unable to hop 5 times on each foot | |

*Lack of limited eye contact*

**Parents** - If there are Red Flags call your Family Doctor or Child Health Nurse
**Professionals** - REFER EARLY – DO NOT WAIT

Article from: https://www.health.qld.gov.au/__data/assets/pdf_file/0015/160701/red-flag-a3-poster-banana.pdf

*Early Childhood Edition*

# Independent Skills

It is our role along with the parents to help teach these little individuals how to become independent beings. At different ages children are capable of different independent skills. Many of these skills need to be explicitly taught so don't just assume they will know how to do it.

|  | 1-2 years | 2-3 years | 3-6 years |
| --- | --- | --- | --- |
| Self help | Attempting to use a spoon and fork independently<br><br>Finding own shoes<br><br>Finding and returning hat to pockets<br><br>Packing away activities | Pull up pants after toileting<br><br>Attempting to dress themselves<br><br>Attempting to put on shoes and socks<br><br>Feeding themselves<br><br>Putting away plates and cups<br><br>Packing away activities<br><br>Cleaning up messes | Dressing themselves<br><br>Putting on shoes and socks<br><br>Serve their own fruit or lunch<br><br>Wash up dishes<br><br>Put artwork into bags<br><br>Make their own beds<br><br>Sweep the floors |
| Hygiene | Hand washing with assistance | Toilet training<br><br>Hand washing with supervision | Toilet independently<br><br>Hand washing independently<br><br>Blows own nose |
| Manners | Reminder to say "Ta," "Please," and "Thank you."<br><br>Say "Hello" and "Goodbye" to people. | Reminder to say "Please," and "Thank you."<br><br>Reinforce saying "Hello" and "Goodbye" to people<br><br>Remind not to interrupt adults when they are talking<br><br>Encourage eye contact when talking to others<br><br>Explicitly teach turn-taking and how to wait patiently for something<br><br>Explicitly teach sharing with others and how we feel if someone won't share | Should only need occasional reminders for saying "Please," "Thank you," "Hello" and "Good bye."<br><br>Teach them to say "Excuse me" when wanting to speak to someone then to wait patiently until they are ready.<br><br>Encourage conversation starters and responses such as "Hi, how was your day at Kindy?" "Great, how was your day at work, Mummy? "What did you do today, Daddy? |

TIPS

"Anyone who does anything to help a child in his life is a hero to me."

**Fred Rogers**

# Organiser

*Teacher for a Day*

# IMPORTANT CONTACT DETAILS

**School/Centre** _____

**Principal/Director** _____

**Address** _____

_____

**Phone** _____

**Email** _____

**Staff Members**            **Phone Numbers**

| Staff Members | Phone Numbers |
|---|---|
| _____ | _____ |
| _____ | _____ |
| _____ | _____ |
| _____ | _____ |
| _____ | _____ |
| _____ | _____ |
| _____ | _____ |

**Fire, Police, Ambulance** _____

**Child Services** _____

**Poisons Information Centre** _____

**State Emergency Services** _____

_____

Early Childhood Edition

# IMPORTANT CONTACT DETAILS

School/Centre _____
Principal/Director _____
Address _____
_____
Phone _____
Email _____

| Staff Members | Phone Numbers |
|---|---|
| _____ | _____ |
| _____ | _____ |
| _____ | _____ |
| _____ | _____ |
| _____ | _____ |
| _____ | _____ |

Fire, Police, Ambulance _____
Child Services _____
Poisons Information Centre _____
State Emergency Services _____

ORGANISER

Teacher for a Day

# SCHOOL YEAR CALENDAR

| Term 1 | Monday | Tuesday | Wednesday | Thursday | Friday |
|---|---|---|---|---|---|
| 1 | | | | | |
| 2 | | | | | |
| 3 | | | | | |
| 4 | | | | | |
| 5 | | | | | |
| 6 | | | | | |
| 7 | | | | | |
| 8 | | | | | |
| 9 | | | | | |
| 10 | | | | | |
| 11 | | | | | |
| 12 | | | | | |
| 13 | | | | | |

Early Childhood Edition

## Record your days or hours worked over the year.

| Term 2 | Monday | Tuesday | Wednesday | Thursday | Friday |
|---|---|---|---|---|---|
| 1 | | | | | |
| 2 | | | | | |
| 3 | | | | | |
| 4 | | | | | |
| 5 | | | | | |
| 6 | | | | | |
| 7 | | | | | |
| 8 | | | | | |
| 9 | | | | | |
| 10 | | | | | |
| 11 | | | | | |
| 12 | | | | | |
| 13 | | | | | |

ORGANISER

Teacher for a Day

| Term 3 | Monday | Tuesday | Wednesday | Thursday | Friday |
|---|---|---|---|---|---|
| 1 | | | | | |
| 2 | | | | | |
| 3 | | | | | |
| 4 | | | | | |
| 5 | | | | | |
| 6 | | | | | |
| 7 | | | | | |
| 8 | | | | | |
| 9 | | | | | |
| 10 | | | | | |
| 11 | | | | | |
| 12 | | | | | |
| 13 | | | | | |

Early Childhood Edition

| Term 4 | Monday | Tuesday | Wednesday | Thursday | Friday |
|---|---|---|---|---|---|
| 1 | | | | | |
| 2 | | | | | |
| 3 | | | | | |
| 4 | | | | | |
| 5 | | | | | |
| 6 | | | | | |
| 7 | | | | | |
| 8 | | | | | |
| 9 | | | | | |
| 10 | | | | | |
| 11 | | | | | |
| 12 | | | | | |
| 13 | | | | | |

ORGANISER

# WORK EXPENSES FOR 20__

**Keep all receipts and this Log Book for Tax Time**

*Tip: Take a photo of receipts and upload to a Tax Receipts App*

| Date | Resources<br>Equipment, Computer and Phones, Materials and Supplies, Stationery, Prizes, Workbag | Shop<br>Officeworks, Kmart etc. | Cost |
|---|---|---|---|
| | | | |
| | | | |
| | | | |
| | | | |
| | | | |
| | | | |
| | | | |
| | | | |
| | | | |
| | | | |
| | | | |
| | | | |
| | | | |
| | | | |
| | | | |
| | | | |
| | | | |
| | | | |
| | | | |
| | | | |
| | | | |
| | | | |
| | | | |
| | | | |
| | | | |
| | | | |
| | | | |
| | | | |

| Date | Clothing<br>Logo only, Protective wear, Sun Protection, Dry Cleaning | Cost |
|---|---|---|
| | | |
| | | |
| | | |
| | | |
| | | |
| | | |
| | | |

Early Childhood Edition

| Date | Professional Development<br>Courses, Costs for Excursions or Camps | Cost |
|---|---|---|
| | | |
| | | |
| | | |
| | | |
| | | |
| | | |
| | | |
| | | |
| | | |
| | | |

| Date | Professional Fees<br>Unions, Registrations, Memberships, Subscriptions | Cost |
|---|---|---|
| | | |
| | | |
| | | |
| | | |
| | | |
| | | |
| | | |
| | | |
| | | |
| | | |

| Date | Travel<br>Travel Expenses, Car Usage, Excursion or Camp Expenses | Kms or Cost |
|---|---|---|
| | | |
| | | |
| | | |
| | | |
| | | |
| | | |
| | | |

| Date | Home Office<br>Phone, Internet and Electricity Usage | Cost |
|---|---|---|
| | | |
| | | |
| | | |
| | | |
| | | |
| | | |

Teacher for a Day

# PROFESSIONAL DEVELOPMENT RECORDS

| Date | Course | Company |
|---|---|---|
| | | |
| | | |
| | | |
| | | |
| | | |
| | | |
| | | |
| | | |
| | | |
| | | |
| | | |
| | | |

Remember to keep certificates, notes and proof of your courses.

*Early Childhood Edition*

| Hours | Standards | Notes |
|-------|-----------|-------|
|       |           |       |
|       |           |       |
|       |           |       |
|       |           |       |
|       |           |       |
|       |           |       |
|       |           |       |
|       |           |       |
|       |           |       |
|       |           |       |
|       |           |       |
|       |           |       |
|       |           |       |

- Find out your Professional Development requirements for your State and ensure you complete the required hours.

- Ask your Principal or Director for upcoming PD and check online for other free and paid courses.

Teacher for a Day

# IMPORTANT DATES

**New Years Day**
January 1

**Australia Day**
January 26

**Chinese New Year**
January 28

**Waitangi Day**
February 6

**Valentines Day**
February 14

**Clean Up Australia Day**
March 5

**St. Patrick's Day**
March 17

**Harmony Day**
March 21

**April Fool's Day**
April 1

**Good Friday**
April 14

**Easter Sunday**
April 16

**Anzac Day**
April 25

**Mother's Day**
May 14

**Red Nose Day**
June 30

**NAIDOC Week**
July 2

**USA's Independence Day**
July 4

**Jeans for Genes Day**
August 4

**Father's Day**
September 3

**R U OK Day**
September 14

**World Mental Health Day**
October 10

**Halloween**
October 31

**Remembrance Day**
November 11

**Hanukkah**
December 13

**Christmas Day**
December 25

**New Year's Eve**
December 31

*Early Childhood Edition*

# SCHOOL TERMS AND HOLIDAY DATES

| 1st Term | |
|---|---|
| Term 1 | Public or other holidays |
| School Holidays | |

| 2nd Term | |
|---|---|
| Term 2 | Public or other holidays |
| School Holidays | |

| 3rd Term | |
|---|---|
| Term 3 | Public or other holidays |
| School Holidays | |

| 4th Term | |
|---|---|
| Term 4 | Public or other holidays |
| School Holidays | |

## Suggested Daily Plans

Routine is an important part of the day for young children in care. It is human nature to be afraid of change and the unknown and our little people are no exception. Routine helps them predict what is coming up and lessens the stress and anxiety that can occur with change and uncertainty. Establishing routines and a regular daily plan will alleviate these stresses, particularly for children new to this environment.

There are some suggested Daily Plans for each age group with accompanying activities in this section. It is to be used as a suggested guide only and to be adapted to your children's needs. Please refer to the activities listed throughout this book for an elaboration on those suggested in the plans.

# Daily Plan and Notes

"Happiness doesn't result from what we get, but from what we give."

Ben Carson

# LEARNING AREA SYMBOLS

Literacy

Maths

Art

Dramatic Play

Music

Outdoor Activities

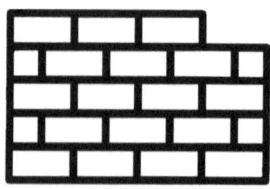
Building

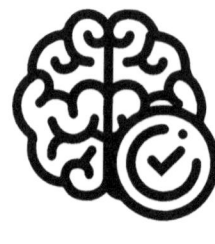
Memory Recall

Science

Gross Motor Skills

Fine Motor Skills

Social and Emotional

Early Childhood Edition

## Daily Plan Template

| | |
|---|---|
| | Opening and setting up |
| | |
| | Morning Tea |
| | |
| | |
| | |
| | |
| | Lunch |
| | Sleeptime<br>Planning, paperwork, and cleaning |
| | |
| | |
| | Afternoon Tea |
| | |
| 5:00 | Prepare for close |

Teacher for a Day

## Babies (0-2 years)

This age group need your tender loving care. Priorities are to ensure the babies are fed, bottled and changed regularly. Check on sleeping babies according to the centre's policy. Monitor babies' interactions and divert their attention if they are upset or getting up to mischief. This plan is a rough guideline as children's ages and needs will ultimately determine how the day will run.

| 6:30 | Opening and setting up |
|---|---|
| 7:30 | Free Play outside<br>  **Sandpit with toy trucks** (pg 204)<br>  **Slide and climbing frames** (pg 164) |
| 8:30 | Ensure babies have had bottles or breakfast if needed and early children have had their nappies changed. |
| 9:15 | Morning Tea |
| 9:30 | Group Time<br>  **Story** (pg 77)<br>Transition<br>  **If Your Name Is...** (pg 65) |
| 9:45 | Indoor Activities<br>  **Play dough with patty pans and candles** (pg 152)<br>  **Ice cube Painting** (pg 125)<br>  **Pom Pom Push** (pg 153)<br>  **Home corner** (pg 172) |
| 10:30 | Pack Away |
| 10:45 | Outdoor play<br>  **Ball Skills** (pg 164) Kicking, catching, and throwing a soft ball<br>  **Water trough with cups and boats** (pg 205)<br>  **Drawing table with crayons** (pg 85) |
| 11:30 | Lunch |
| 12:00 | Sleeptime<br>Planning, paperwork, and cleaning |
| 2:00 | Indoor Activities<br>  **Puzzles** (pg 103)<br>  **Books** (pg 77)<br>  **Duplo Block Play** (pg 135) |
| 2:45 | Group Time<br>  **Nursery Rhymes** (pg 189)<br>Transition<br>  **Identify It** (pg 66) |
| 3:00 | Afternoon Tea |
| 3:30 | Outdoor Play<br>  **Slide and Climbing Frames** (pg 164)<br>  **Cars** (pg 206) |
| 5:00 | Prepare for close |

Early Childhood Edition

## Toddlers (2-3 years)

This age group is so cute but can be very demanding. They are figuring out their place in this world, trying to assert themselves and find their independence. This means toddler tantrums, toilet training and regular fights over toys. They need quite a bit of assistance and lots of modelling with how to do an activity. There is constant mediation and help with teaching them how to share, communicate and get along.

|  |  |
|---|---|
| **6:30** | Opening and setting up |
| 7:30 | Free Play outside<br>   **Sandpit with small boxes, cartons, containers and utensils** (pg 204)<br>   **Bikes and Cars** (pg 206)<br>   **Teddy Bear's Picnic** (pg 206)<br>   **Large wooden blocks with animals** (pg 135) |
| 8:30 | Ensure children have had breakfast if needed and early children have had their nappies changed. |
| **9:30** | Morning Tea |
| 10:00 | Group Time<br>   **Story** (pg 78)<br>   **Doggy, Doggy Where's Your Bone?** (pg 182)<br>Transition<br>   **Five Fat Sausages** (pg 67) |
| 10:15 | Indoor Activities<br>   **Play dough with tools** (pg 156)<br>   **Painting on rocks with toothpicks** (pg 123)<br>   **Train tracks** (pg 156)<br>   **Pet shop** (pg 173) |
| 11:00 | Pack Away |
| 11:15 | Outdoor play<br>   **Hula Hoops** (pg 165) Crawling through, jumping in and out of |
| **11:45** | Lunch |
| **12:15** | Sleeptime<br>Planning, paperwork, and cleaning |
| 2:00 | Indoor Activities<br>   **Puzzles** (pg 103)<br>   **Book Nook** (pg 78)<br>   **Alphabet blocks** (pg 134) |
| 2:45 | Group Time<br>   **Action Songs** (pg 184)<br>Transition<br>   **Partners** (pg 66) |
| **3:00** | Afternoon Tea |
| 3:30 | Outdoor Play<br>   **Sandpit** (pg 204)<br>   **Cars and bikes** (pg 206) |
| **5:00** | Prepare for close |

Teacher for a Day

# Kindy (3-4 years)

This age group is when friendships start forming and they are becoming more independent. They have a longer attention span to participate in activities and better understand how to share and play with their peers, although monitoring is still essential. Learning should be centred around their interests and be in a more incidental through play, games and utilising teachable moments.

| | |
|---|---|
| **6:30** | **Opening and setting up** |
| 7:30 | Free Play outside<br>**Sandpit with pots, pans, teapots, tea cups, cutlery and utensils** (pg 204)<br>**Obstacle Course** (pg 163)<br>**Ten Pin Bowling** (pg 206)<br>**Fairy Garden** (pg 206) |
| **9:30** | **Morning Tea** |
| 10:00 | Group Time<br>**Story** (pg 79)<br>**Musical Chairs** (pg 182)<br>Transition<br>　**Find your name** (pg 66) |
| 10:15 | Indoor Activities<br>**Play dough with nature items** (pg 156)<br>**Nature collage using leaves, twigs, shells, bark etc.** (pg 126)<br>**Stick Threading** (pg 153)<br>**Stacking objects using rocks and blocks** (pg 135) |
| 11:15 | Pack Away |
| 11:30 | Outdoor play<br>**Skipping rope** (pg 163) Balancing on, jumping either side, walking |
| **12:00** | **Lunch** |
| **12:30** | **Sleeptime**<br>**Planning, paperwork, and cleaning** |
| 2:00 | Indoor Activities<br>**Puzzles** (pg 103)<br>**Drawing with pencils** (pg 155)<br>**Match card game** (pg 96) |
| 2:45 | Group Time<br>**Counting Songs** (pg 187)<br>**Who's Missing** (pg 96)<br>Transition<br>**I Spy** (pg 66) |
| **3:00** | **Afternoon Tea** |
| 3:30 | Free Outdoor Play<br>**Sandpit** (pg 204)<br>**Cars and bikes** (pg 206) |
| **5:00** | **Prepare for close** |

Early Childhood Edition

# Pre School (4-6 years)

This group can work more independently and should be encouraged to think more critically through open ended questioning. They will be creating friendship circles but some may need help and encouragement in this area on how to make friends, share and cooperate with others. Teaching can be more intentional and structured but most of the learning should still be implemented through play and adapted as an extension of their interests to make learning meaningful in their world.

|  |  |
|---|---|
| 6:30 | Opening and setting up |
| 7:30 | Free Play outside<br>   **Sandpit with small cars and cardboard ramps** (pg 204)<br>   **Cubby house with soft toys and dress ups** (pg 207)<br>   **Tennis racquets and balls** (pg 206)<br>   **Office setup with keyboards and desks** (pg 173) |
| 9:30 | Morning Tea |
| 10:00 | Group Time<br>   **Story** (pg 79)<br>   **ABC Jump** (pg 84)<br>   **Alphabet Hunt** (pg 83)<br>Transition<br>   **Find the matching lower case letter** (pg 84) |
| 10:30 | Indoor Activities<br>   **Science Experiment- Flying Paper Planes** (pg 144)<br>   **Paper Tracing** (pg 87)<br>   **Trace a Shape** (pg 106)<br>   **Paper Ball Toss** (pg 155)<br>   **Archaeologists** (pg 173) |
| 11:30 | Pack Away<br>Grouptime<br>   **Pizza Massage** (pg 198) |
| 11:45 | Outdoor play<br>   **Yoga** (pg 164) |
| 12:30 | Lunch |
| 1:00 | Rest time<br>Planning, paperwork, and cleaning |
| 2:00 | Indoor Activities<br>   **Puzzles** (pg 103)<br>   **Book Nook** (pg 79)<br>   **Threading** (pg 155) |
| 2:45 | Packaway<br>Group Time<br>   **Story** (pg 79)<br>   **Who Stole the Cookie From the Cookie Jar?** (pg 183)<br>Transition<br>   **Wibbly Wobbly** (pg 66) |
| 3:00 | Afternoon Tea |
| 3:30 | Free Outdoor Play<br>   **Slides and Climbing frames** (pg 164)<br>   **Bikes and Scooters** (pg 206) |
| 5:00 | Prepare for close |

Teacher for a Day

# Daily Outdoor Set Up

Kids love being outdoors. They love discovering and exploring new things so it is important to change the outdoor setting regularly to keep children engaged and inquisitive in this learning area.

Often you will have many outdoor activities set up. Below is just an example of activities to focus on each day to ensure there is a variety of skills being practised both inside and outside.

|  | MONDAY | TUESDAY | WEDNESDAY | THURSDAY | FRIDAY |
|---|---|---|---|---|---|
| **Gross Motor** | Bikes (pg 206)<br><br>Hoops (pg 165) | Obstacle Course (pg 163)<br><br>Climbing (pg 164) | Skipping rope (pg 163)<br><br>Parachute (pg 208) | Climbing (pg 164)<br><br>Hopscotch (pg 165) | Ball Skills (pg 164)<br><br>Sport Time (pg 206) |
| **Fine Motor** | Drawing (pg 155) | Cutting (pg 155) | Threading leaves (pg 155) | Water Play (pg 205) | Play dough with plastic animals (pg 156) |
| **Creative Arts** | Spray Bottle Painting (pg 124) | Play dough with nature bits (pg 127) | Nature Art Painting on rocks (pg 126) | Chalk drawing on the pavement (pg 122) | Fishing Rod Painting (pg 123) |
| **Dramatic Play** | Teddy Bears Picnic (pg 206) | Home corner in the sandpit (pg 204) | Fairy Garden (pg 206) | Office set up (pg 207) | Cubbyhouse (pg 207) |
| **Building** | Large wooden blocks with stuffed animals (pg 207) | Lego with small animals (pg 207) | Plastic blocks in the sandpit (pg 207) | Small blocks with cars (pg 207) | Make a river (pg 137) |
| **Other** | Literacy<br>Object Hunt (pg 97) | Music<br>Musical Instruments (pg 207) | Science<br>Flying Paper Planes (pg 144) | Maths<br>Matching and sorting leaves (pg 110) | Sustainability<br>Watering cans for plants (pg 214) |

## Daily Outdoor Set Up

|  | MONDAY | TUESDAY | WEDNESDAY | THURSDAY | FRIDAY |
|---|---|---|---|---|---|
| Gross Motor | | | | | |
| Fine Motor | | | | | |
| Creative Arts | | | | | |
| Dramatic Play | | | | | |
| Building | | | | | |
| Other | | | | | |

Early Childhood Edition

# CRITICAL REFLECTIONS

As educators we need to reflect in our practise as well as reflect on our practise.

Critical reflection is a comprehensive, multi-layered way of analysing an experience. It is an important part of our role as educators and is a learned skill that requires practise.

**There are multiple levels of reflection-**
- Own experiences, ideas and knowledge
- Different perspectives, experiences and knowledge of others
- Relevant literature and theories
- Wider social and political influences such as policy changes, stereotypes and societal beliefs.

It is not enough to only use our own interpretations and experiences as this will result in a more surface-level reflection. As educators, we need to add a range of perspectives and resources to our analysis to ensure a detailed and critical reflection is occurring to improve children's outcomes. Effective critical reflection will help you understand what occurred and why, and bring about changes of practise if necessary.

Critical Reflections require courage to step outside your normal thinking patterns, preconceived ideas and expectations. We need to question what we are doing and why. We need to read and refer to literature to support our thoughts or to deepen our knowledge. Understand that other people have different backgrounds, culture, values and practises to what we do. Does society's "norm" apply to this child? Are we listening to the children?

---

**Ask yourself questions like-**
*Who is advantaged when I work in this way?*
*Who is disadvantaged?*
*How well do I understand each child?*
*Have I taken time to talk to each child to find their interests and likes?*
*What am I challenged or confronted by?*
*Is there some literature that could help me better understand*
*what I have observed?*

---

Ultimately children, parents and educators will benefit from deeper reflections about professional practise. When we have a culture of professional inquiry that continually reviews current practises, reflects on outcomes and generates new ideas then the wellbeing and success of the children will be at the forefront of their practise.

Teacher for a Day

# NOTES

Early Childhood Edition

# NOTES

Transitions are an important activity to implement in your day to create order and routine and are a great way to add in some intentional learning. Use these when moving from an activity to hand washing and eating, from a group time to activity time or from group time to outdoor time.

These transitions are a great way to make a child feel important when they are called out and chosen for the next task and it encourages confidence and self-assurance in getting up in front of the class.

# Routine and Transitions

"What we learn with pleasure,
we never forget."

**Alfred Mercier**

Teacher for a Day

# DAILY ROUTINE SONGS

## Morning Songs

**Make a Circle**
Make a circle
Make a circle
Big and round
Big and round
Everybody hold hands
Everybody hold hands
Now sit down
Now sit down

**Days of the Week
(sung to The Addams
Family theme song)**
Days of the Week
(Clap, clap)
Days of the Week
(Clap, clap)
Days of the Week,
Days of the Week,
Days of the Week!
(Clap, clap)

There's Sunday
and there's Monday
There's Tuesday
and there's Wednesday
There's Thursday
and there's Friday
And then there's Saturday!

Days of the Week
(Clap, clap)
Days of the Week
(Clap, clap)
Days of the Week,
Days of the Week,
Days of the Week!
(Clap, clap)

**Good Morning to You**
Good morning to you
Good morning to you
Good morning to
(name or dear friends)
It's nice to see you!

**Tell Me What Your Name Is**
Tell me what your name is I
wonder if you know?
Your name is ___
(Point to child and they say
their name)___
Hello, hello, hello, hello, hello,
hello, hello. (While waving to
them).

**Bee Bee Bumble Bee**
Bee bee bumble bee
Can you sing your name
to me?
My name is (name).
(child sings)
Good morning (name).
(everyone sings)

**Hey Good Morning**
Hey good morning,
ho good morning
What a lovely day
Hey good morning,
ho good morning
Won't you come and play
Hey good morning,
ho good morning
Clap your hands in time.
Hey good morning,
ho good morning _____
your hands like mine!
(Insert action here such as
wave, flap, touch, slap, click,
fold)

**Where is _____?
(Sung to Where is
Thumbkin?)**
Where is (name)?
Where is (name)?
Here I am (child sings)
Here I am (child sings)
How are you today friend?
Very well thank you
(child sings)
Have a great day
Yes I will (child sings)

TRANSITIONS

*Early Childhood Edition*

## Goodbye Songs

### Where are the Children? (Sing to Where is Thumbkin?)
*Where are the children?
Where are the children?
Here they are, Boo!
Here they are, Boo!
We had fun at (Kindy).
We had fun at (Kindy).
Bye for now.
Bye for now.*

### It's Time to End the Day (Sing to Farmer in the Dell)
*It's time to end the day
It's time to end the day
It's time to say a big hooray
And then be on our way.*

### This is the Way We Say Goodbye (Sing to Mulberry Bush)
*This is the way we say goodbye
Say goodbye, say goodbye
This is the way we say goodbye
At (Kindy) each day.

We give our friends a big high five
A big high five, a big high five
We give our friends a big high five
Then we say goodbye!*

# TRANSITION

## Transition Games

- **Actions**
Call out a child at a time and give them an action to do as they move off to their task.
They could hop, jump, crawl, tip toe, shuffle, walk backwards, frog jump, skip, side step, walk on their knees etc. This is also great practise for their gross motor skills.

- **Go if You're …**
Send children off by different characteristics such as-
  - colours they are wearing,
  - types of clothing (long pants, shorts, dress, skirt, socks)
  - colour, type or length of hair
  - age
  - birthday month
  - name starts with a …

- **If Your Name Is…**
If your name is _____, please stand up
If your name is _____, go wash your hands.

## Transition Games

**I Spy**
Play I Spy to send children from a group time to an activity. "I Spy with my little eye, someone wearing a tutu/name starts with…/has curly hair." That child can then move off to wash hands, go to an activity or go outside.

**Partners**
Children can choose a partner to take to an activity. You could ask them to choose someone of the opposite sex or someone they don't usually play with to encourage new friendships. Be mindful to observe those children that often don't get chosen and ask them to choose someone first on occasion.

**Identify It**
Extending from what they are learning get children to identify a colour, shape, toy, picture, animal, letter, number or word to then move to the next activity. You could get them to tell you what "this" is OR get them to point to or find "this".

**Find your Name**
Write on the board or use name tags and children need to find their name for the transition.

**Wibbly Wobbly**
Children need to listen for the word that rhymes with their name.

*Wibbly wobbly woo, an elephant sat on you.*
*Wibbly wobbly Warah, an elephant sat on …Sarah!*

**Spelling Names**
For the older children working on name recognition try spelling their name out aloud and they need to recognise their name to move to their next task.

Early Childhood Edition

## Transition Songs

Choose some children to stand up in the front. Sing the song and as one or more is eliminated in the song they move off to the next task. Then get up another group of children and repeat.

### Five Currant Buns
Five currant buns
in the baker's shop
Round and fat with
a cherry on top
Along came a boy
with a penny one day
Bought a currant bun
and took it away

(Repeat alternating boy and girl)
Four/Three/ Two/ One currant bun in the
baker's shop…

### One Grey Elephant
One grey elephant balancing
Step by step
on a piece of string
They thought it was such
a wonderful stunt
That he called
for another elephant.

(Repeat)
Two/Three/Four/ Five grey elephants balancing…
…
That he called
for another elephant.

But what do you think happened?
They all fell off!!!

### If You're Wearing
(sung to Mary had a Little Lamb)
If you're wearing
(blue/socks/pants) today,
Blue today, blue today.
If you're wearing blue today
Stand up and shout "Hooray!"

### Five Cheeky Monkeys Swinging in the Tree
Five cheeky monkeys
swinging in the tree
Teasing Mr Crocodile
"You can't catch me,
you can't catch me!"
Along comes Mr Crocodile
as quiet as can be
And… SNAP!

(Repeat)
Four/ Three/ Two/ One…
cheeky monkey swinging
in the tree…

### Ten in the Bed
There were ten in the bed
and the little one said
"Roll over, roll over!"
So they all rolled over
and one fell out

(Repeat)
There were nine/eight/seven…

### Five Little Duck
Five little ducks went out
one day
Over the hills and far away
Mother duck said
"Quack, quack, quack."
But only four little ducks
came back.

(Repeat)
Four little ducks went out one day…

### Five Cheeky Monkeys Jumping on the Bed
Five cheeky monkeys
jumping on the bed
One fell off and bumped
its head
Mama called the doctor
and the Doctor said
"No more monkeys
jumping on the bed!"

(Repeat)
Four/ Three/ Two/ One…
cheeky monkey jumping on
the bed…

### Five Fat Sausages
Five fat sausages
frying in a pan
All of a sudden one went
"BANG!"

(Repeat)
Four/ Three/ Two/ One…
fat sausage frying
in the pan…

### Three Jellyfish
Three jellyfish
Three jellyfish
Three jellyfish
sitting on a rock
One fell off
Argh!!!

(Repeat)
Two/One jellyfish…

TRANSITIONS

Teacher for a Day

# 🎒 PACKING AWAY IDEAS

It can be tricky getting young children to pack away. It is beneficial to give warning in advance to help them wind their activity down and transition in their minds from play time to pack away time.

**Cues**
You can use different cues to signal to the class that it is pack away time. You want to limit raising your voice over the noise so some of these strategies are effective.

Pack Away song

Shaker

Bell

Gong

Play some music

Turn off the lights

**Cleaning Time**
Get little brooms, dustpans and brushes and cloths and watch how eager the children will be to help clean up.

**A Clean Race**
Designate areas for children to tidy and make it a race to see who cleans their area the quickest.

**Tidy Tongs**
Put out tongs that children need to use to pick up toys. This seems like fun to them and also works on their fine motor skills.

**Magic Item**
Tell them you have chosen a "Magic Item" and the person that tidies it up will get a stamp/sticker/get to be the line leader etc. Keep the game going until all the room is cleaned up then reveal who picked the Magic Item.

**Model**
Young children need to be shown how to clean and tidy up. Show them where the toys go, how to wipe the table, how to sweep the floor. Young children often love helping out so use it to your advantage and show them how to do it properly so you don't have to redo it!

**Cleaning Freeze**
Add a little fun to clean up time and call out "Go" for them to start cleaning then randomly call out "Freeze" then "Go" again. This can make it easy to spot those actually packing away and give you a chance to praise those children and encourage the others not helping out as much.

Early Childhood Edition

### Magical Roleplay
Cast a spell on your class to become a busy bee, robot maid, rubbish collector or vacuum cleaner etc. and get them to act out the roles to tidy the room.

### Simon Says
Play Simon Says to get children to help pack away. "Simon says, pack away the blocks." "Simon says, pick up the rubbish on the floor." "Go play outside. I didn't say Simon says!"

### Star Cleaners
Tell the class the best helpers will get a stamp or sticker. The room will be spotless in no time!

### Beat the Buzzer
Set a timer and get children to race against the clock to get the room tidy. Watch them move quickly to get it done.

## Pack Away Songs

### The More We Help Together (Sing to The More We Get Together)
*The more we help together, together, together*
*The more we help together the happier we will be.*
*'Cause your toys are my toys and my toys are your toys*
*The more we help together the happier we will be.*

### Time to Clean Up
*Now it's time to clean up*
*Clean up, clean up*
*Now it's time to clean up*
*Let's all do our share.*

### Pack Away
*Pack away, pack away*
*Everyone help pack away!*

### This is the Way We Pack Away
*This is the way we pack away, pack away, pack away*
*This is the way we pack away, when we've finished playing.*

### It's Time to Pack Away (sing to Farmer in the Dell)
*It's time to pack away*
*It's time to pack away*
*Finish what you're doing*
*It's time to pack away.*

### Pick it Up and Pack it Up
*Pick it up and pack it up*
*put it all away*
*Pick it up and pack it up*
*Play another day*

TRANSITIONS

# NOTES

Early Childhood Edition

# NOTES

TRANSITIONS

Pre-Literacy skills are an important facet to learning and it starts as soon as they are born through the simplest of actions.

**Talking** develops their language skills and stimulates their brain development.

**Singing** to children particularly with rhyme helps develop their decoding skills as they learn the sounds of letters and word patterns.

**Playing** is how young children learn about the world. The more they learn the easier it will be to read and understand reading down the track.

**Reading** is deemed the most effective way to help children become good readers.

# Literacy

"Keep reading. It is one of the most marvellous adventures that anyone can have."

**Lloyd Alexander**

Teacher for a Day

# BABIES & TODDLERS
## Pre-Literacy Skills

- Reading lots of books to the children will help develop a love for reading and increase their vocabulary. Be sure to point out objects, repeat sounds, words and colours.

- Letting them read and explore books.

- Give them magazines to scrunch, rip, kick and play with.

- Sing songs and do actions.

- Drawing with different tools- textas, pencils, chalk, crayons (especially the broken stubby ones as they are great for fine motor skills).

# 3-6 YEARS
## Pre-Literacy Skills

**Rhyming Books**
Choose rhyming books to practise similar sounding words. They can predict words using rhyming patterns:
"The cat sat on the mat wearing a hat."
"The big pig will do a jig in a wig."

**Alphabet Search**
Identify the letters of the alphabet.
Use a chart, chalk on the ground, letter on the board, letter cards or a puzzle. Make it a competition or turn-taking activity. "Who can find the g first?" Use a smaller amount of letters depending on their ability.

**Alphabet Detective**
Hide letters around the room and the children need to be detectives to go and find them. Tell them they need to come back and tell the teachers what letters they found in order to work out the hidden message.

*Early Childhood Edition*

## 3-6 years

**Collage a List**
Get children to collage in a list format, a grocery list for the week. Discuss healthy and unhealthy choices. Younger children could have pre-cut shopping items to glue in and older children can cut their own from magazines or brochures.

*Extension*
Give children a notepad to write their own list.

**Lists**

*Discussion*
Explain that a list is a group of items written down the page to tell us information. Discuss examples of a list and its purpose (shopping lists, class list, to do lists, daily routine etc.) and choose one for them to help you create. Use pictures and words to help explain it.

**Repetitive Books**
Children love anticipating what comes next so books like "Brown Bear, Brown Bear, What Do You See?" "There Was An Old Lady Who Swallowed A Fly" and "We're Going On A Bear Hunt" are always hugely popular and helps with their reading confidence. Praise and encourage their "reading" and predicting because if a child feels a sense of mastery and power they will be more willing to try.

**Open-Ended Questioning**
This style of questioning encourages the child to give a full, meaningful answer rather than a simple Yes or No.

What, how, why, when, where questions are great for this rather than do, is, are, could, should questions.

Some questioning examples could be-
- Where did you go on the weekend?
- What did you eat for dinner last night?
- How do you feel today?
- When are you going on holidays?
- Why were you feeling sad?

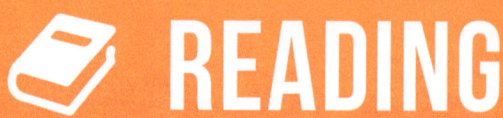

## Reading Strategies

It is important to explicitly teach reading strategies and you can start as early as 2 years with some of these. Model these strategies by thinking out loud.

### Predicting/Inferring
Get children to predict what the book is about, what is going to happen next, what will the ending be? These skills help engage the reader, activate their prior knowledge and make connections with the text.

### Summarising the Main Idea
Get children to retell what happened in the story in their own words. Encourage sequencing words such as first, second, next, last. This will show understanding of the text. Ask them- Who? What? Where? When? Why? How?

### Clarify
Are there any tricky words or concepts that need to be explained?

### Evaluate
What did you think about the text? Did you like it? Why?
What did you learn?

### Making Connections
Text to Self- What in this book reminds me of myself?
Text to Text- What in this text reminds me of another story?
Text to World- What in this text reminds me of things in the real world?

## Questioning

Questioning helps you check for understanding and is key to develop their reading comprehension skills. There are three types of questioning-

### Literal
This is the more straight forward questioning with the answers found directly in the text.
*What colour was the car? What was the boy's name? How old was the girl?*

### Inferential
These questions are trickier as you need to work out what the text means. There can be more than one answer for these questions and it checks for deeper understanding. They need to look for clues and read between the lines.

Ask questions like -
*How did she feel? How do you know that? What words make you think that?*

Other inferential questions could be -
*Why did...? How did they feel? What is the problem? What did they mean by...? Why did the character...? What lesson does this teach?*

### Evaluative
These questions are using their own ideas. They are thinking critically to make their own judgements about the text.

Evaluative questions could be -
*What do you think about ...? Do you agree with the character? How could you fix the problem?*

Early Childhood Edition

## 0-2 years

At this age they are beginning their pre-reading skills. They might play with books, open them and turn pages and even point to words mimicking reading. They will enjoy looking at bright colours and pictures and love hearing you read to them. They may even start to learn their alphabet usually through song.

**Touchy-Feely Pre-Reading**
Give babies and toddlers access to a variety of reading materials. Books (use feely board books for babies), magazines, catalogues, newspapers. Let children touch, kick at to explore the sounds and even rip at the disposable reading materials. Point and name different pictures, letters and words as they look at them.

**Noisy Stories**
Get picture books that emphasis sounds. Animal or vehicle books are great for this. Point to the pictures and make clicking, choo-chooing, quacking or roaring sounds and encourage them to mimic your sounds.

**Familiar Faces**
Create a book using pictures of educators, friends in the class or family members for the children to look through. They will love identifying people that they know and love.

**Story Telling**
Read lots of different types of books for children to listen to and interact with. Use lots of facial expression and actions. Being read to is the single biggest factor to improving intelligence so don't underestimate the humble story telling.

**Interesting Read**
If they are a child that loves trucks, get them lots of vehicle books, extend a child that loves dogs with books about pets, jungle or farm animals. If you can find what they love they will engage and learn more readily.

LITERACY

Teacher for a Day

## 2-4 years

At this age children will be practicing pre-reading skills. They will often mimic reading and even make up stories when flicking through a book. They will start to understand the difference between different characters such as a letter, a number and a picture. They will start to identify words and symbols that are familiar in their world e.g. their name, their age or popular signage e.g. McDonalds. They will become familiar with the alphabet song and will start to recognise some letters.

**Story Telling**
Read lots of different types of texts (big books, picture books, websites, magazines, newspapers, letters, posters, postcards) for children to listen to and interact with. Use lots of facial expression and actions.

**Nursery Rhymes**
Nursery Rhymes are a fabulous way to enhance reading skills. Use them to identify rhyming words, clap out syllables and deconstruct to find the meaning and hidden lesson. Find Nursery Rhymes on page 189.

**ABC**
Sing the ABC's and point to each letter on a poster/whiteboard as you go. Get children to come and point to letters they can identify.

E.g. Can you find the first letter of your name? What letter does Dad start with?

**Predict It**
Use a familiar book and as the story progresses get them to predict what will happen next. Prompt them if needed. This skill helps engage the reader, activates their prior knowledge and making connections with the text.

**Name Tags**
Children love when they can recognise their own name, so make name tags for their lockers, your morning board, placemats for eating or something where they need to find their own name. Praise them for reading their own name and see if they can start identifying each other's names.

Early Childhood Edition

## 4-6 years

At this age children will become Beginner Readers. They may memorise books and reread them over and over and often use picture cues to help them read. They should be recognising letters, many sounds and will be attempting to read simple words. They should start to differentiate and match upper and lower case letters. They may identify the initial sound in a word then make the rest up if unsure.

Start off with familiar words such as their name, Mum, Dad, sibling and venture into CVC words (explained on page 82). Using rhyme is a great way to find common word families and reading patterns.

**Tons of Texts**
It is great to expose children to lots of different types of texts. Use big books, picture books, non-fiction books, websites, magazines, newspapers, letters, posters, postcards, brochures, cereal boxes, etc.

**Look it up**
Use the internet to research topics the class is interested in. Look at and read the webpages and print out important information to display in the classroom.

**Read for Pleasure**
Encourage children to read for pleasure. Set up a cosy book nook with appealing books. Allocate different times for them to go there, you could even use a timer to give it more appeal. Igniting a love for reading is paramount at this young age.

**Story Sequencing**
After reading a story get children to retell the story in sequence using the language first, second, next, then, finally etc. Draw boxes and fill them in with the children's responses or get photocopies and shrink pages of the book for the students to cut, glue and sequence themselves.

*Teacher for a Day*

## 4-6 years

*A tisket, a tasket*
*Here is the rhyming basket*
*Match the words that sound the same*
*That's how we play the rhyming game*

**Rhyming Basket**
In the middle of a circle place a basket with a designated word family -eg -og. Then using rhyming word cards or rhyming and non-rhyming objects, children need to decide what words DO rhyme then place them in the basket. Say the following poem as they take turns to find the matching words to put in the basket.

**Rhyme It**
Give students a word and they need to come up with a word that rhymes with it. It can be a real or nonsense word. You can write it on the board or just do it verbally.

**Box**- fox, socks, locks
**Sad**- mad, dad, rad, jad
**Hot**- lot, snot, spot, smot
**Trumpet**- crumpet, lumpet, mumpet

**Find the Rhyme**
Using a rhyming book or poem get children to predict and identify the next word that rhymes and will make sense in the text.

*Early Childhood Edition*

## 4-6 years

**Syllable Clap**
Breaking words into syllables is a great way to segment words for ease of reading and later on for spelling. All words are made up of syllables. Start by going around the circle clapping out each child's name in syllables. Then try other words as a class, clapping out syllables of things they can see in the room. Write some words up to show them the syllables and how they are segmented.

Tramp- o - line   Al- ex –an- der

**Super Pointer**
Make a large pointer out of a stick or ruler to use when reading to the class. Then get students to make their own "Super Pointer" by decorating the end of a paddle pop stick. Show the children how it works, teaching them about one-to-one correspondence. You could do a series of activities with this depending on their developmental stage.

Progress with pointing from left to right of the following things in a line-

• objects such as toys, cars or books

• sticker dots on a page

• spaced out numbers (in or out of order)
  3 8 5 2 1 9
• spaced out letters (out of order)
  f  o  t  p  z  m  c

• close together letters (out of order)
  spjlwx
• spaced out simple words
  cat  it  dad  run

This should help them understand that one string of letters makes up one word. Let them take them home to practise with their parents when you are done with them in class.

**LITERACY**

# LETTER WORK

**Letter sounds**
There are many programs to teach this. For most children to learn their sounds it takes a lot of repetition, so try and make it fun.
Use YouTube songs to practise.
Use flash cards and repeat the sound and any funny rhyme that could accompany it.

It is preferable to teach letters and letter sounds out of order so that children aren't too fixated on the ABC's song structure to identify letters. Give purposeful and meaningful exposure to letters every day. When playing with letter blocks, looking at posters or reading a book ask what the letter is or what does that word start with. If you want a "Letter of the week" to focus on, choose 2 or 3 letters instead in order to expose them to as many letters as possible. 26 weeks or half a school year is a long time to get through the alphabet so condensing will help get through them faster, especially when some children may already know some of their letters.

## 3-6 years

**Rhyme It**
Rhyming words are a great way to build on familiar word families.
Brainstorm words that rhyme with **cat, bug, net, hit, mop, duck** etc.

**CVC Words**
These are the basic words to start with that have a Consonant-Vowel-Consonant pattern. Only choose words that are phonetically correct e.g. **cat, top** or **bug** not **saw**.

**Creative Letters**
Make letters with pipe cleaners, buttons, string, sticks, rocks and any other craft goodies you can find. Twist, bend, glue and shape the material into different letters.

**Letter Find**
Teacher writes out the alphabet then students need to identify the correct letter with the teacher's clues.

Examples:

Letter that comes before…

Circle the letter between…

What are the next 2 letters after…

Underline the 3rd letter.

What are the previous 2 letters before…

Cross out the 15th letter.

Early Childhood Edition

## 3-6 years

**Sound Sort**
Have objects starting with two different letter sounds. Get children to sort into their correct sound groups.

**Missing Sounds**
Choose a focus sound to work on. Students fill in the missing letter to complete the word. Teacher or children then draw a picture of the word.

**Alphabet Hunt**
Using alphabet cards or a written alphabet, hide the letters around the room or yard. If possible hide them with items starting with the same letter, e.g. Letter P with the Pencils. Children go on a hunt and then need to bring the card back to the middle and match it with the letters on the mat. You can do this by matching the same letters OR matching upper and lowercase letters together.

**One Day I Went Walking…**
Students sit in a circle and they are given an alphabet letter. Everyone could have the same letter, a choice of 2 letters, the same letter as their name or use the whole alphabet. They need to think of a word starting with that letter and going around in a circle answer "One day I went walking and saw a…ball."

### 3-6 years

**Eye Spy**
Play "Eye spy with my little eye, something beginning with…F" to teach and reinforce letter sounds.

**ABC Jump**
Spread the alphabet cards out or write in chalk on the ground and take turns having them jump on the letter or sound that you call out.

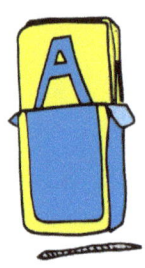

**Alphabet Card Games**
With a pack of alphabet cards children can play Snap, Memory or letter tracing with baking or tracing paper.

**Letter Case Matching**
Glue foam letters or just write letters on to a paddle pop stick then in a box cut slits and write the lowercase letters for the child to match them.

> *Extension*
> More advanced students can try to spell out words by choosing the right letters and placing them in the slots.

🟧 Blends   🟥 Word Families

| bl | br | ch | ck | cl | cr | dr | fl | fr | gh |
|----|----|----|----|----|----|----|----|----|----|
| gl | gr | ng | ph | pl | pr | qu | sc | sh | sk |
| sl | sm | sn | sp | st | sw | th | tr | tw | wh |
| wr | ack | ain | ake | ale | all | ame | an | ank | ap |
| ash | at | ate | aw | ay | eat | ell | en | est | et |
| ice | ick | ide | ight | ill | in | ine | ing | ink | ip |
| it | ock | oke | op | ore | ot | uck | ug | ump | unk |

**Onset and Rime**
Onset refers to the initial consonant sound or blend and rime refers to the vowel and final consonants sounds. This skill is one of the most effective ways to enhance phonological awareness. You can do this through practicing word families and exploring consonant sounds and blends.

> *trip*
> **tr** is the onset
> **ip** is the rime

# WRITING

*Early Childhood Edition*

Prewriting skills are important for reading and writing success. It is also important to practise fine motor skills in order to aid them in developing their writing skills.

The writing development generally starts at scribbles that they do not distinguish as any different from drawing. They then move on to making separate 'marks' that symbolise their writing, showing their understanding between written and illustrated work. These markings then develop into horizontal and left to right directional writing before evolving into alphabetical symbols.

## 0-2 years

At this age children are developing their prewriting skills. A lot of work on their fine motor skills will help with this. Also refer to page 151 for more fine motor activities.

**Cotton Tip Painting**
Get children to paint using cotton tips on paper, alfoil or any other desired surface. Great for fine motor skills.

**Drawing in Sand**
Either in a sandpit or a container with sand, encourage children to draw and make patterns in it. You could use paddle pops sticks, small sticks, end of a spoon or paintbrush to help draw squiggles.

**Drawing**
Give children lots of different supplies to draw with (not all at once!). Pencils, textas, crayons, chalk, pastels, charcoal, stamps, highlighters, fingers. Broken, stubby crayons are particularly great for their fine motor skills. Let them draw on coloured paper, newspaper, magazines, whiteboards, concrete, balloons, paper plates or cups.

Teacher for a Day

# PRE-WRITING LINE DEVELOPMENT

Before attempting to write letters children should master these shapes first. Ask them to draw or trace lines and shapes relevant to their age and skills. The ages are a developmental guideline of mastery.

### 3 years

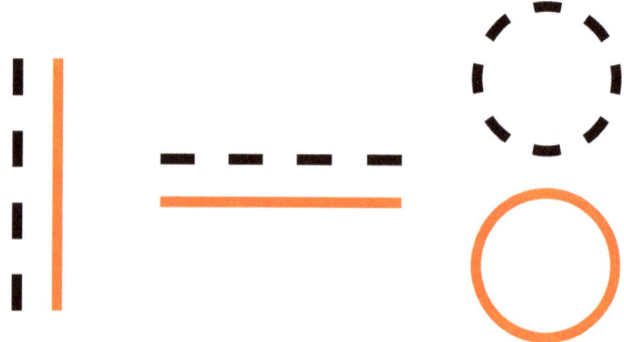

### 4 years

### 5 years

Early Childhood Edition

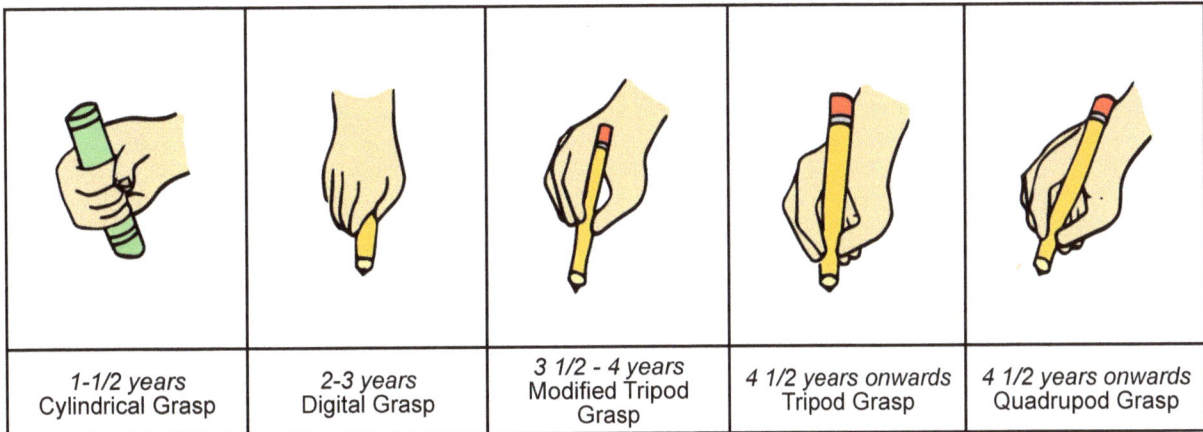

### Pencil Grasps
Encourage and teach the children the correct pencil grasp. You are aiming for them to be using a Tripod or Quadrupod Grasp.

### Highlighter Tracing
Write the child's name with a black marker and give them highlighters to trace the letters of their name.

### Dot to Dot
Use 5-6 dots per letter and write out the child's name with a marker. Get them to join the dots and hopefully identify their name.

### Tally Marks
Introduce the concept of tally marks and that one line equals one. Put objects in front of the children and get them to write tallies when counting the objects.

### Cotton Tip Painting
Using the pincer grip to hold the cotton tip and painting with it will help them build up strength in their fingers and practise their pencil grip.

### Laminated Tracing
Get a tracing font off the internet and laminate words for them to trace with whiteboard markers. Start off with their own names and expand into other CVC or simple words.

### Paper Tracing
Give students tracing or baking paper to trace names, letters, numbers, shapes or pictures (colouring in books can be great for this). Show them how it is easier to see what you are tracing if you hold it up to the window to let the light pass through behind.

LITERACY

Teacher for a Day

**3-6 years**

**Draw a Monster/Clown Poem**
Students follow the poem's instructions to draw each character.

**Draw a Monster**

When you draw a monster, it is said
You must begin with a funny-shaped head.

He'll be able to see in the night skies
If we draw him three googly eyes

Our monster will have a big, ugly nose
With green boogers coming out like a hose

He needs a mouth so he can eat
All the children's smelly feet

Now up the top and underneath
This monster needs lots of sharp teeth

Just below we need to check
 That we don't forget to draw his neck

 Our monster is big and his belly is too
  So let's draw his large body blue

 To make him look a little scary
 He needs some arms that are hairy

 Some legs are needed
 to make him move
 Choose how many to make him groove.

 To help him walk down the street
  He will need some big, stinky feet

  Now it's time
  to make your monster unique
  Add something scary that will make everyone shriek!

*Early Childhood Edition*

**3-6 years**

**Draw a Clown**

When drawing a clown it is said
You must begin with his
big round head

He wants attention
so people will stare
So give him colourful, curly hair

He wants to hear people
laugh and cheer
So on each side of his head
give him an ear.

To make sure he can see what to do
Draw for him bright eyes, coloured blue

We can't forget what everyone knows
Is he must have a red, round nose

His mouth is as wide as
the River Nile
So draw for him a
humongous smile.

Draw his body,
his arms and hands
Add orange gloves that look so grand

He needs some legs to help him stroll
Make them long and skinny like a pole

Draw him an outfit that looks mighty fine
He loves a onesie with a colourful design

For his feet, here's some clues
He needs some big, goofy clown shoes

On his shirt he wears a trick flower
If you get too close it will give you a shower

I hope you listened to every rule
And now your clown is looking cool.

**LITERACY**

Teacher for a Day

# SPEAKING AND LISTENING

Children need to learn language skills in order to communicate with others. Listening, speaking and thinking skills are often overlooked and need to be explicitly taught.

Oral language is the foundation for learning and important for future learning. Children need good modelling of speaking and listening.
- Practise good articulation of words and emphasise tricky sounds such as s, r, th and sh.
- Demonstrate how to use manners in conversations and how to have discussions by asking others questions such as How was your weekend? Do you like that? What would you like to play?
- Practise conversational skills as well as performing skills by speaking in front of the class and projecting their voices.
- Demonstrate and practise the use of inside voices, outside voices and whisper voices and when you may need to use them.

Model good listening skills where their body is still, eyes are on the speaker, ears are listening and mouth is not talking. Teach children how to listen and respond when spoken to and how to wait their turn to speak once the other person has finished talking.

These simple things may seem obvious to us but it is important we are teaching them these basic skills for them to be successful communicators in the future.

## 0-2 years

**Picture Cues**
Use picture cards or posters and talk about the names of the picture and what sounds they make. Animal, transport and other sounds tend to be the easiest for young children to pick up so start with them.

## 0-2 years

### Action Songs
Singing action songs is a great way for young children to listen, sing a long as well as copy actions. See page 184 for action song examples.

Open, shut them

Open, shut them

Give a little clap.

Go and get me a book.

### Following Instructions
Develop the children's working memory by giving them 1 step instructions such as- *"Go get me a book." "Put your hat on." "Point to the dog."*

If they are capable, extend into 2 step instructions such as *"Go to the toilet and wash your hands," "Get the block and put it in the bucket," "Show me the tree and the sun."*

Can you find the toy bear?

### Peek-a-boo
Playing peek-a-boo has so many developmental benefits. From 5 months old babies can start to develop object permanence- where they understand that just because they can't see an object doesn't mean it does not exist. So hiding your face, whole body or an object, then reappearing reinforces this skill. Peek-a-boo also develops visual tracking, gross motor skills, social development plus they find it hilarious.

Hide behind something and jump out or hide something under a towel or a box and let them search for it.

## 3-6 years

*Clap-clap-click-clap-clap-click*
*Stomp-clap- stomp- stomp-clap*

**Sound Patterns**
Get children to repeat sound patterns that you make using clapping, clicking, knee slapping, stomping, tapping etc.

**Follow the Leader**
The leader heads a line and leads the group around doing different actions as they go, jumping, hopping, clapping etc. Teacher starts off then can appoint students to take over.

**Do What I Say, Not What I Do**
Children need to listen carefully and follow your directions.

Teacher says *"Do what I **say**, not what I **do**. Put your hands on your head (while you put your finger on your nose.)" "Clap your hands (while you stand on one foot)."*

Watch the students getting confused and slowly start to listen and pay attention more. When they have mastered that, change it up and say- *"Do what I **do**, not what I **say**. Flap your arms (while you put your hands on your hips.)" "Sit on your hands (while you touch your toes)."*

*Early Childhood Edition*

## 3-6 years

### Simon Says
Teacher says a direction and the students need to follow, but only if they say *"Simon Says."*

*"Simon says, put your finger on your nose."*
*"Put your hands on your knees."* If children put their hands on their knees then you caught them out.

### Tongue Twisters
*I scream, you scream, we all scream for ice cream.*

*Peter Piper picked a peck of pickled peppers.*

*She sells seashells by the sea shore.*

*How much wood would a woodchuck chuck if a woodchuck could chuck wood?*

*Fuzzy Wuzzy was a bear. Fuzzy Wuzzy had no hair. Fuzzy Wuzzy wasn't very fuzzy, was he?*

### Opposites
Use picture cards or draw pictures of opposites. Children need to find and match the opposites- big/small  tall/short  fat/thin  in/out  up/down  soft/hard  left/right  inside/outside  light/dark  hot/cold  new/old  young/old  full/empty  clean/dirty  happy/sad  here/there  night/day  wet/dry  strong/weak  heavy/light

*Teacher for a Day*

### 3-6 years

**Follow Directions**
Give children directions to find things for you around the room or in the yard. *"Go and find a leaf." "Go and find a red toy car."*

Then try two or three step directions. *"Go and get a leaf then put it in that bucket." "Go and find a car, put it in the container then put it on the table."*

**Draw Directions**
Get students to draw a picture using Directional Words.

*Draw a tree in the **middle** of the page. Next draw an orange sun **above** the tree. Draw a red flower **below** the tree. Draw a yellow and black bee **on** the flower.*

At the end discuss why there were so many differences in everyone's pictures even though everyone was given the same instructions.

**Find the Opposites**
Get children to find or show you the opposites when you call out a word.

*Find something hard/small/up/in/under/heavy*

**Be the Teacher**
Even from a young age children can be experts in an area they are interested in.
As an alternative to Show and Tell get them to Teach and Explain something to the class that they know a lot about. It might be counting in a different language, the names of the dinosaurs or how to dress yourself.

*Early Childhood Edition*

# 🧠 MEMORY AND RECALL

Having a good memory is key for success with future schooling and learning. Memory activities can help children master the skills of organising, storing and recalling information. Working memory allows you to remember things in action so that you can remember the steps in a familiar recipe, helps you to read fluently and helps your mathematical skills. Weak working memory will restrict learning ability so it is essential to teach and develop memory skills from a young age.

## 0-2 years

**Where Is?**
Using posters, photos or books ask the child to find something. Use the same stimulus again and again and see how much quicker they can find the object.

**Routine**
Establish a routine with key cues so the children can remember what is to come next. Use bells for meal times, songs for packing away or washing hands.

**Packing Away**
Teach the children where the toys and activities live so they can remember and help clean up at pack away time.

**Silly Dressing**
Play a silly game where you put your hat, shoe or sock on your knee, hand or elbow and watch how the young children find it hilarious all the while testing their memory of where the clothing should go!

**Name It**
Once they start talking get them to name different objects by holding up the object or a picture. This helps them recall and remember the words and images together.

**Songs**
Teaching young children songs such as Action songs and Nursery Rhymes helps them with their memory and recall.

**What Sound?**
Ask the child *"What sound does a… duck/dog/car/dinosaur make?"*

Teacher for a Day

## 3-6 years

**Categorise It**
Put different toys into colours or features then get them to add a new toy to the correct category. This helps them to remember certain traits for different toys.

**Learn a Poem or Song**
Get children to learn a popular poem or song to recite in front of the class.

**Who's Missing?**
Children need to spread out around the room and tuck into a ball. One child will be covered with a sheet and when the class is asked to sit up they need to pick who it is that is hiding under the sheet.

**Pick the Missing Object**
Put different items in the middle of the circle. Children need to observe and remember them. Put some cloth over them and take one item away and then they need to recall what is missing.

**Story Recall**
After reading a book get children to verbally retell the story then get them to draw a picture of what happened or what the character looked like.

**Memory Match**
Using memory match games are a great way to practise and enhance their working memory as they need to remember where cards are placed in order to win.

### 3-6 years

**Morning Routine**
Routines can be an easy way to work on memory skills. A morning routine that discusses the weather, days of the week, date, children present, months of the year, ABC's, counting, songs and any other basic skills helps reiterate the learning intention as well as helps them predict and remember important information.

**I Went to the Shop**
Children sit in a circle and name things that they bought at the shop. Each student has to recall what the previous students have said.

*"I went to the shop and I bought…an apple."*
Next *"I went to the shop and I bought… an apple and cake."*

**Object Hunt**
Draw up a list of things the children need to collect either in the room or out in the yard. They need to try and remember the items and how many they need to collect. Encourage them not to return to the board too many times to check the list to try and encourage their memorising skills.

# NOTES

# NOTES

Becoming numerate in the Early Years is the ability to make connections to mathematics in the real world. We need maths in our everyday lives to build a lego tower, read the movie timetable, share our treats equally with friends, bake a cake, work out how to get to a friend's house or buy a toy from the shop. So, in order to teach numeracy we need to make it relevant to their little lives.

Some concepts of focus are **Number Recognition, Counting, One-to-One Recognition, Counting on and Back, Patterning, Sorting and Classifying.** Other Maths concepts that can be addressed include **Measurement, Shapes, Directions, Time, Money and Problem Solving.**

The teaching of numeracy needs to be simplified and make sense in their world. Ask questions like *"How many…" "How much…" "Which is bigger or smaller?" "What is heavier or lighter?" "Which has more or less?"* By regularly asking these questions, it will allow them to better understand the concepts and see its importance in their world.

# Numeracy

"Tell me and I forget.
Teach me and I remember.
Involve me and I learn."

Benjamin Franklin

# Maths for 0-2 years

Maths in a young child's world should be informal and encouraged through play and their own life experiences. This is easy to address through counting everything and anything, identifying shapes around them or playing with puzzles and nesting games. When building towers use measurement language such as tall, short, big and small. When they are helping pack away get them sorting the toys or discuss heavy and light objects they are carrying.

### Fill Them Up
Get children to explore capacity by filling up different sized cups or bowls with water or use different sized boxes and containers to fill with sand or dried pasta etc. Use language such as full, half full and empty.

Then try filling the container with pingpong balls or another object. Is it full? What if we add in rice or sand? Now is it full?

### Patterns in the World
Look at different patterns around you such as *a zebra's stripes, tiles, a leaf, the fence.*

### Shapes
Practise naming shapes, counting their sides, doing shape puzzles, playing with shape sorters and discussing shapes in their world.

*Look the ball is round.*
*That window is a rectangle.*
*The toast is a triangle.*

### Size Them Up
Get the children to explore length by identifying the bigger/smaller, taller/shorter/longer item out of two different objects. Ask a child to go find the biggest or smallest rock/car/ball/teddy they can find.

### Colour Sorting
Give the children 2 different coloured balls or blocks to sort into a matching colour container.

### Block Tower Patterns
Demonstrate growing patterns by putting one block, followed by two (one on top of the other), then a tower of three then four blocks. Get the child to copy this pattern.

### Nesting Game
Get nesting toys or other toys or containers that fit inside each other. This game teaches them about size differences and solving problems through logical reasoning.

Early Childhood Edition

**Counting in their world**

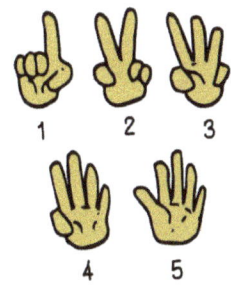

- Practise counting 1-10 so they understand the order of the numbers.
- Count toys, pictures in a book, pencils, people, toes, shoes or anything they can touch.
- Count using your fingers so they can begin subitizing.

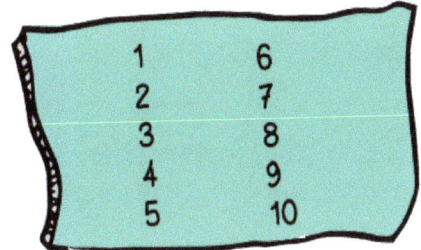

- Show them numbers from 1-10 so they can identify the word with the numeral.
- Count to 3, 5 or 10 both forwards and backwards to do an action such as jumping or going down a slide.

NUMERACY

**Puzzles**
Puzzles are a great maths activity to explore shape, size and area. It develops their fine motor skills, enhances cognitive development and visual spatial awareness. It is great for problem solving, hand and eye coordination, social skills and promotes self-esteem and perseverance through the small successes each time they fit a piece in.

**Object Sorting**
Get children to sort different objects into containers.

They could sort-
*Leaves and rocks. Flowers and sticks. Cars and dolls. Wooden blocks and Duplo blocks.*

You can even turn it into a packing away activity!

**AB Patterning**
Make and discuss patterns with things like coloured blocks, dot stickers, coloured paddle pop sticks etc. You could then stick the patterns onto paper.

**Tall Towers**
When playing with blocks get the child to build a tower and use language such as tall, big and high. Build a small tower next to it and explain that it is small, little or short. Ask them to make the tower bigger, taller or higher. See if they can build it taller than the chair or than themselves. Get them to knock it over and start again to encourage the skill of persistence and perseverance when things go wrong.

**Matchy Matchy**
Get children to match objects by their look, colour, size, shape or texture. Doing this by using their world around them makes maths and learning more meaningful. Ask them *"Can you find me one the same as this."*

You could try matching the following-
- Shoes or socks in the shoe box
- Same coloured hats, balls or blocks
- Balls, blocks, books or cars that are the same size
- Use blocks and balls to match shapes
- Soft toys and figurines to match soft and hard.

Teacher for a Day

## Maths for 3-6 years

Teaching Maths can be more purposeful with the older children but still must be relevant and fun for them to be able to understand and relate to it in their world.

# COUNTING

Counting is an integral part of Maths and an essential building block for numeracy. By 3 years they should be starting to identify numerals and counting from 1-10+. Be sure to expose children to number words as well as numerals.

**Dice Stamping**
Using dice and paint, get children to press the dice into paint then press on to the paper. They can count the dots or subitize them, then write the number next to it if capable.

For more capable children they can stamp two dice side by side and add the total.

**Tallying**
Introduce tally marks and how we use them to count objects. Get children to count and tally up different items- pencils, teddy bears, girls, boys etc. Don't introduce the rule of 5 straight away until they have fully grasped the concept.

## Counting One-to-One

Learning how to count using one-to-one correspondence is the most important step when counting.

- Practise by counting people in a line, touching their heads one at a time.
- Count people in the class discussing how many are here today.
- Counting objects such as teddy bears, cars, chairs for musical chairs.
- Progress to touching items one at a time in a line on a page then to random pictures on a page.
- Get children to count how many animals are in the picture, how many pages in the book, how many photos on the wall etc.
- Practise counting in a circle making sure they are mindful of their starting point.
- Move on to counting items in a more jumbled array.

## Subitizing

Subitizing is the skill of seeing how many objects are there without counting. For example you can easily know all the numbers on a dice without actually counting them.

Put up your fingers to show a number and get the students to tell you how many it is, without counting. Explain that what they did is called "subitizing." Next show pictures and get children to hold up their fingers as quickly as possible how many they think it is without counting them. Then move on to dots. Show them the dot formation on a dice then move on to dots in a random array.

### Extension
*Introduce a tens frame with dots and demonstrate that 10 is the whole frame and how we can count on from 5, count back from 10 and easily subitize using this tool.*

## Dice Dots

Draw or print rows of dots on a page, the amount is up to you. Next roll a dice, circle that many dots then write the number in the circle. You can play this individually, in pairs, in groups or as a whole class.

Teacher for a Day

# SHAPES

Shapes are all around us and one of the first things we teach children. Shapes are used to observe, categorise and compare objects. It reinforces the simple concept of same and different. As children become familiar with regular 2D shapes, then more confident with irregular shapes you can start introducing shape attributes such as the number of sides, corners, edges and then move on to 3D shapes.

### Shape Pictures
You can use blocks to dip in paint and stamp on paper. Encourage children to create a picture with the shapes.

*A circle for a sun.*
*A square and a triangle for a house.*

### Shape Sorting
Discuss the names of the shapes, number of sides and whether the edges are curved or straight. Get children to sort different shapes into different categories.

• *Same amount of sides*
• *Curved or straight edges*

### Trace a Shape
Use different shape blocks and children can trace the block, identify the shapes and count the sides.

### Shapes in Our World
Discuss and get students to identify different shapes in our world.

*Pizza is a circle, a book is square, a door is a rectangle, an egg is oval, a piece of cake is a triangle.*

Get them to go on a hunt to find different shapes around the room and report back to the class with what they found.

*Early Childhood Edition*

# PATTERNS

Patterning is an important intelligence skill that helps make predictions, enhances problem solving skills and works on pre-algebraic skills.

### Growing Patterns
Explore growing patterns by building towers. Start off with one block, followed by two blocks, then three, four, until it all falls down. Then try to do the same growing pattern with buttons, cars or counters.

They can then create their own Growing Pattern Art by gluing on sequins, buttons, patty pans or small paper squares.

### Repeated Patterns
With blocks, coloured counters, or any other objects show repeated patterns.
Do an ABAB pattern using different colours, sizes, shapes or objects and get them to copy and continue the pattern then try to make up their own.

As an extension explore ABBABB patterns or ABCABC patterns or fill in the missing pattern.
*ABAB- Blue, pink, blue, pink…*
*ABBABB- Big, small, small, big, small, small…*
*ABCABC- Square, circle, triangle, square, circle, triangle…*
*Missing pattern- Teddy, car,_____, car, teddy…*

### Pattern People
Try this once children are familiar with what a pattern is. They can play spot the pattern once you have put the children into the pattern yourself.

Sort them into patterns that they need to identify using-
*Gender, shoes, hair colour, eye colour, clothes, expressions etc.*

### Movement Patterns
Introduce patterning in a physical way using movement by putting the children into a line using different types of patterns. You can shape their body into different movements then get them to predict what will come next-

*Sit, stand, sit, stand, sit…*
*Hands up, hands on hips, arms out, hands up, hands on hips, arms out…*
*Finger on nose, touching toes, touching toes, finger on nose, touching toes…*

Use this when children are familiar with patterning. They can play spot the pattern once you have put the children into the pattern yourself.

### Pattern Jewellery
Children can make patterned necklaces or bracelets using string, wool or pipe cleaners and threading coloured pasta, fruit loops or coloured beads using a simple repeated pattern.

## Missing Patterns

Create a pattern that is missing an object. The children need to decide which object they need from a variety of objects, to make the pattern complete.

Bat, ball, bat, ball, _____.
Pencil, crayon, pencil, _____, pencil.
Circle, triangle, _____, triangle, circle, _____.

Children can then create their own pattern and get a friend to finish it off for them. This could be a physical pattern, a drawing, cut out shapes or pictures, coloured painting or objects.

## Symmetry

Symmetry is the same as a mirror image. Explore the line of symmetry in our world. *Leaves, blocks, cars, honeycomb, flowers, spiderwebs, snowflakes, sun and more.* Can they see any things that are symmetrical? Ask them if different things are symmetrical or not.

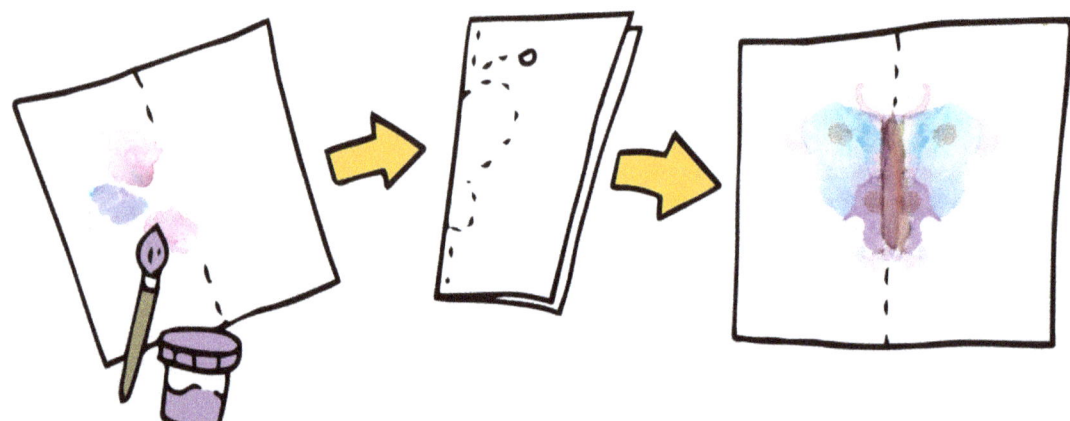

## Symmetry Art

Get children to do "Butterfly Art" where they fold a piece of paper, then put some blobs of paint on one side then fold the page back in half, smoothing down the page to smoosh the paint together. Open it back up to reveal the symmetrical picture. Does it look like anything? What did they notice happened?

*Early Childhood Edition*

# POSITIONAL AND DIRECTIONAL LANGUAGE

This language is an important life skill to master and is easily implemented in everyday language and activity. Explicit teaching and direction of some of this language is needed to help them completely understand the concept.

## Directional words

| | | | | |
|---|---|---|---|---|
| above | after | around | before | beginning |
| behind | below | beside | between | bottom |
| down | end | far | finish | front |
| in | inside | left | middle | near |
| next to | off | on | out | outside |
| over | right | start | through | top |
| under | up | upside down | | |

### Directional Words
Discuss and demonstrate different Directional Words (list above). Have a chair in front of the group. One at a time, give students instructions to demonstrate their understanding of the different directions.

*Sit **on** the chair. Crawl **under** the chair. Stand **next to** the chair. Put the ball **over** the chair. Put the teddy **behind** the chair. Children can then do it themselves with a <u>cup</u> and a small <u>object</u> following the teacher's directions.*

*Extension*
*Children can do it to each other, taking turns to give directions to their partner.*

### Directional Maze
Set up a maze that the children need to get through using cushions, chairs, books etc. One at a time give them instructions to get through the maze by using directional language. Then get them to do it in pairs. If you're game you could get them to do it blindfolded.

*Take two steps **forward**, step **over** the book, crawl **under** the chair, go **around** the cushion, side step **left** till you get to the bookshelf.*

Take 2 steps forward... Step over the chair... Go around the cushion...

NUMERACY

**Following Directions**
Get students to draw a picture using Directional Words.

For simpler drawings try-
*Draw a circle in the **middle** of the page. Put a cross **above** the circle. Put a wiggly line under the circle. Draw a face **in** the circle. Write your name at the **top** of the page.*

For more advanced ability try-
*Draw a tree in the **middle** of the page. Next draw an orange sun **above** the tree. Draw a red flower **below** the tree. Draw a yellow and black bee **on** the flower, etc.*

At the end discuss why there were so many differences in everyone's pictures even though everyone was given the same instructions.

**Positional numbers**
Ask children if they can show you what first and last is. Set up a race for a couple of children to demonstrate their prior knowledge. Ask them if they know what second, third or fourth means. Show them the correlating numbers that go with each place.

Next do silly races where some children race and the other children are the judges and give the place numbers out. The races could be hop, crawl, skip, frog jump, walk backwards, tip-toe, slow motion etc. The judges hold a 1st, 2nd, 3rd, 4th, 5th place cards and hand them to the competitor as they cross the finish line.

# MATCHING AND SORTING

Once a child is matching more than two objects they are now sorting. Sorting is when someone is comparing and determining the similarities and differences and how to group them. These skills are an integral step in progressing onto more complex maths tasks as well as developing life skills such as sorting cutlery, groceries, laundry, money etc.

**Objects to Sort**
Give children containers, ice cube trays, tongs, baskets or boxes to sort their objects into.

Money

Leaves

Buttons

Coloured pencils/ crayons/textas

## Graphing

Get the children to sort objects into different categories OR ask them a question and record their answers to then be graphed.

### For sorting

- Blocks into their shapes
- Toys into soft and hard
- Their shoes into sandals, thongs or runners
- Books into soft and hard covers
- Food into healthy/unhealthy or fruit, vegetable, dairy, meat, bread.

### For interviewing/questioning

- Favourite animal
- Favourite ice cream flavour
- Favourite food
- Favourite game

Now you can record the answers in a Tally Mark chart. Start off with just the lines and introduce the tally 5 concept down the track.

| Shoes | Tally Marks |
|---|---|
| Laces | IIII |
| Velcro | III |
| Buckles | I |
| Zipper | II |

In the same lesson or try it in another lesson if it is too much, you can then make a physical graph on the ground using string or chalk. Add the labels on the graph and students can add an object (e.g. shoe) or a picture of their response (e.g. chocolate ice cream) to the right column in the graph. Explain that this is a form of "Picture Graph." Ask questions such as "Which has the most/least?" "How many does ____ have?" "How many more ____ than _____ are there?"

### Extension

*You can then get them to create a picture graph from your recorded information in the Tally Chart by drawing or sticking pictures onto a graph template.*

Teacher for a Day

# MEASUREMENT

The use of non-standard measurement is an essential step before moving into standard measurement such as centimetres and litres. In the younger years it is an imperative building block for their skills.

## 3-6 years

**Line Them Up**
Using different sized objects, get the children to order them from smallest to largest or largest to smallest. You could use the same objects or a combination of different things such as cars, feathers, leaves, sticks, rocks, pencils, crayons, scissors, ruler etc.

**Get in Order**
Put the class in order from shortest to tallest. Get them to try and do it themselves. You could start by getting the children to find someone taller or shorter than them and stand in front or behind.

**Family Portrait**
Get children to draw their family in order of tallest to shortest.

**Same Same or Different**
Give students 2 or 3 objects to compare from to identify whether they are taller/shorter/longer, bigger/smaller, heavier/lighter or whether they are the same.

Ask students to find an object shorter than, longer than and the same as for e.g. a pair of scissors. They then need to explore the room to find something to suit.

They can bring these things back to the circle or trace these things onto paper into the appropriate column.

**Towers**
Build with blocks to make tall towers and encourage them to build one taller than themselves or the chair.

Early Childhood Edition

**Measure Me**
Measure parts of their body such as a foot or a hand by tracing on to paper. Then, using paddle pop sticks/unifix/ matchsticks or some other non-standard unit of measurement, get them to explore and count how many units long the outline is.

After observing their measuring skills, have a discussion about the ways they measured their outline. Did they measure the length or the width? Did they space out their measurement unit, overlap it or have it just touching? Discuss whether that would change our answer.

Explain that one object = one unit of measurement. Demonstrate with two different sized outlines how you can measure them to find out which is longer however, use different sizes, gaps or overlaps to test their understanding, e.g. use big and small paperclips or space out unifix on one and join them together on the other. Would this affect our answer? Why? What should we do to make it fair?

*Extension*
*Measure your body height by tracing an outline around your body onto large butcher's paper. Introduce the concept of measuring using hand spans and get them to measure how many hand spans tall they are. Discuss the different answers when different people measure the same outline due to their different sized hands.*

**How Long Is Your Name?**
Give an example on the board of two names in the class. Choose a long and a short name. When you write them up write the long name skinny and squished up and the short name fat and long. Then ask what name is longer and encourage a discussion about the differences in the number of letters and the way they are written. Hopefully they will identify that the letters need to be the same size.

Next use grid paper or boxes for the students to write in or have the children's names typed out or in boxed letter cut outs so they are all one standard size. Ask the children to stick the names in order of shortest to longest down the poster and compare the lengths between the names and explain how the boxes keep the letters the same size and why that is important.

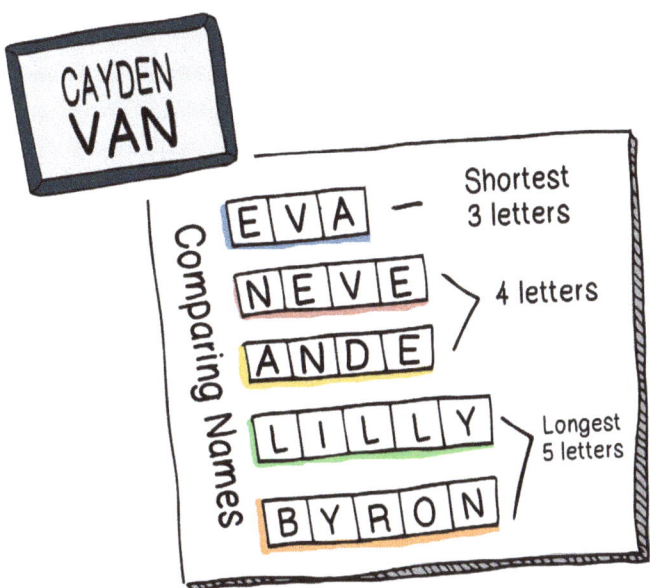

*Extension*
*Get students to cut out and design different objects from a strip of paper and order them from tallest to shortest or shortest to longest.*

*You could cut up strips of newspaper to be redesigned as high rises or a strip of plain or coloured paper could become a snake.*

NUMERACY

## Balancing Act

Using a balance introduce the concept of weight by explaining how heavier things will go to the bottom, lighter things will go to the top. If they weigh same or similar it will be straight/level. Use the seesaw as a practical example of a balance then get students to act like a balance when holding one heavy item in one hand and a light item in the other.

Demonstrate how the balance works. Get children to predict whether it is a heavy or light object and compare two objects to see which is heavier or lighter.

### Extension
*Using a non-standard measurement such as unifix blocks or pop sticks get children to predict how many blocks would weigh the same as a glue stick for example.*

## Marble Capacity

Explore capacity by predicting how many marbles or pom poms it would take to fill the jar then count them to find out the exact amount.

## Block Area

Use unifix blocks, MAB, or other small blocks to measure the surface area of two similar objects that are different in size e.g. a leaf. Get them to predict which one is bigger and will need more blocks to cover it. Covering the object as best as they can they are then to count how many blocks there are to find the area of each object. Discuss the similarities of the object and how their measurements are different.

## Volume

Show the children a variety of containers (choose long and skinny, short and wide, long and narrow) and ask them to compare them and predict which containers would hold more. Explore with water in a water trough by filling up one then pouring it into another. Did it overflow? Did it hold more or less water than you predicted?

## Choose your Measurements

Get children to explore the measurement of an object such as a book, a table, a mat, the slide etc. using a non-standard unit of measurement. Supply them with a "Messy Measurement Box" to choose their measurement items such as string, paper squares, unifix, pop sticks, paperclips, wool, etc.

Discuss why they chose their items for measuring and compare with others their discovery.

Early Childhood Edition

# TIME

In the younger years, learning time isn't so important as understanding the concept of time. This can include days, dates, weeks, months, years along with hours and minutes. Children often want to know how long it is when they have to wait 5 minutes? How long until night time? When will it be tomorrow? When is my birthday?

### Days of the Week
This can be incorporated into your morning routine. Talk about today's day, what day was it yesterday and what day will it be tomorrow. Practise the days of the week through song (refer to page 64).

### Seasons
Visuals are a great way to teach months and seasons. Explain what the season is for each month and incorporate it into your morning routine.

Recite with the class-
*Today is Monday. Yesterday was Sunday. Tomorrow will be Tuesday. The month is September. The season is Spring.*

### Months
Go through the months of the year as a class. Talk about birthdays and who shares the same months. You could collect this information, record it with tallies then graph it with the children using their photos or birthday cakes to represent them in the picture graph.

### Dress for the Season
Discuss what you would and wouldn't wear for the different seasons. Have a teddy that you dress appropriately during each season.

### Season Themes
As the seasons change incorporate the theme into your art and craft and daily planning.

*Summer-* Water play, teach sun safety.
*Autumn-* Art with fallen leaves, leaf paint printing using autumn colours
*Winter-* Collage a snowman using cotton balls, make snowflakes by cutting folded white paper.
*Spring-* Collage flowers by scrunching up and gluing on coloured crepe paper, folded butterfly symmetry art.

# NOTES

# NOTES

Art encourages imagination, freedom of expression, problem solving, spontaneity and play. It can appeal to different children's learning styles and it can help children with physical, emotional or behavioural needs.

Art promotes creativity, helping children to become better thinkers, which is something we need more of in the world. It can be a multisensory experience, enhancing neural connections. Art can also help to build their fine motor skills and can be the foundation for writing. But most of all, art is a fun and enjoyable way to learn all of these skills and more.

# Art

"Make each day your masterpiece."

**John Wooden**

# Different Types of Art Supplies to Use

**Washable acrylic paint**

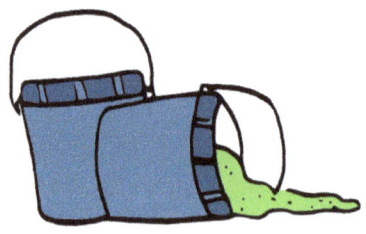
**Powdered water paint**

**Water colours**

**Charcoal**

**Pastels**

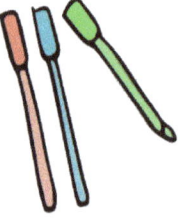
**Textas**

**Pencils**

**Crayons**

**Chalk**

Early Childhood Edition

# Things to Use Instead of Paper

- Aluminum foil
- Baking paper
- Sand paper
- Leaves
- Rocks
- Bark
- Balloons
- Newspaper
- Magazines
- Catalogues
- Windows or glass doors
- Paper plates
- Paper doilies
- Napkins
- Paper towel
- Material
- Cardboard

## All Ages — Alternative painting ideas without a paintbrush

**Blocks**
Use different shaped blocks then dip them in paint and press onto paper. They could identify the shapes or use them to create a picture using shapes.

**Rubber Gloves**
There are always plenty of rubber gloves around so you could blow them up, fill them up with sand, rice or water and get children to do finger painting with someone else's finger!

 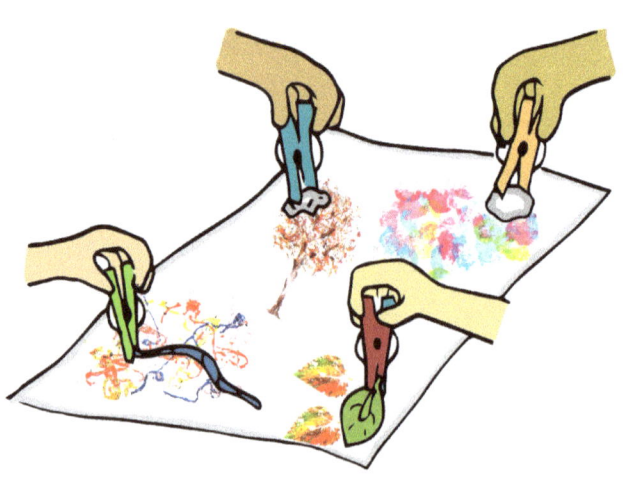

**Bubbles**
Using bubbles or detergent combined with water paint and water in a cup, get the child to blow bubbles in the water through a straw until it is overflowing on to the paper, staining the paper with its colours. Not recommended for the younger children.

**Pegs**
Use pegs to hold on to the end of various objects to then use as a paintbrush. You could use cotton balls, pipe cleaners, aluminium foil, sponge, bubble wrap, pom pom balls, string, leaves, ribbon etc.

**Toothpicks**
Toothpicks can be great to do fine art work such as painting dots for Aboriginal artwork or for swirling and mixing paints together onto paper to make fine patterns.

**Utensils**
They could use forks, spoons, spatulas, whisks or any other kitchen appliance available to them. A dish scrubbing brush is particularly effective, especially for painting trees.

**Fishing Rod Painting**
Make fishing rods using a stick and string or wool. Then get children to dip the string into the paint and flick it onto the paper on an easel.

**Candles**
Using candles and water paints you can do a wax resistant painting. Just draw a pattern or picture or write their name with the candle onto paper then paint over it with water paints and watch the picture become visible.

# ART

Teacher for a Day

**Marbles**
Put marbles in a tray or box and roll the marbles through blobs of paint.

**Cars**
Using the wheels of the car to drive through blobs of paint on paper.

**Food**
You can use cut up fruit and vegetables to stamp and paint with. Apple and potatoes are ideal for carving out shapes to use as stamps. Citrus fruit is good to cut in half and use to stamp with. You could experiment with any type of food for painting with, or on to!

**Spray Bottles**
Put water colour paint into spray bottles and let them paint (outside) onto large sheets of paper. Be sure to have something on the ground and on them to avoid stains.

**Tools**
Children can use nuts, bolts, and screws to dip in paint and press onto paper.

**Paint Pens**
Paint pens, fabric paint or puff paint can be a fun change and can usually be found cheap at the dollar store.

**Feathers**
Substitute the paintbrush with a feather. They can experiment using both ends.

**Fingers, Toes, or Body**
Messy fun and inevitable with the young ones. Use different body parts to paint with or on to!

**Ice Cube Painting**
Freeze water paints into ice cube trays with toothpicks or paddlepop sticks to hold them then paint and experiment as they melt onto the paper.

**Fly Swatter**
Put paint in a tray and use a fly swatter to paint with. It can be messy so be sure to use large paper, aprons on and preferably do it outside.

# Nature Art

Go for a nature walk to find items in the landscape to use for art. Children can do amazing things with leaves, rocks, grass, flowers, bark, tree nuts, pinecones, reeds and many other wonderful things in nature.

Make interesting patterns with pinecones or tree nuts by rolling it in paint then on the paper.

Tie flowers and leaves to the ends of sticks and use them like a paintbrush. Or more simply just use a flower like a paint brush.

Paint a flower or leaf and press it onto the paper. Observe the features of the plant on the paper.

Put a flower or leaf underneath paper and do crayon rubbings over the top of it.

Paint on rocks using fabric or puff paint.

Use long reeds or grass to paint with. Children can "whip" the paper using different coloured paints (careful observation needed for safety reasons).

Make a collage using leaves, flowers, grass, shells and other natural delights.

Either with a hole punch or just a pencil children can punch a hole through a leaf and then thread it on to string to make a necklace.

Get children to thread leaves, shells, wooden beads and other natural objects onto a piece of string. Tie the string on to a stick to make a beautiful hanging ornament.

Early Childhood Edition

ART

Using a picture shaped hole punch, get children to punch holes through a leaf and use the picture cut outs to collage on a page.

Find some decent sized twigs in your surroundings. Place them in play dough to make them stand up right then the children can thread beads onto the branches to create a decorative mini tree.

Design leaf people, houses, flowers, a nature scene or anything else their hearts desire using bits and pieces from nature.

Use nature bits such as tree nuts and seeds to roll and make impressions into play dough.

Use clear contact for children to stick natural craft on to decorate.

Create a sculpture using sticks, stones and other bits and pieces.

Get ground spices from the pantry and tip into containers. Get the children to smell them and tell them the names of the spices. Add a little water to them with paintbrushes and let them paint. Get them to smell the "paint" and their page and see if they can remember which spices they were.

Paint with a brush onto a flower, rock, pinecone, bark, leaves or anything else they come across in nature.

Make designs in the dirt or sandpit using sticks.

# DRAWING

### Shadow Drawing
Set up different objects, figurines, blocks and shapes outside on a piece of paper. Children can then trace the shadow and see their design.

### Squiggles
Draw squiggles all over the page and get the child to colour in each different section with a different colour.

### Directed Drawing
You would be surprised how well young children can follow your directions to create a drawing. Draw a simple picture, step by step, and get them to follow your instructions.

Early Childhood Edition

### Colour Tracing
Give children a picture from a colouring book to trace with baking paper or tracing paper. Then get them to colour the picture in.

### Tracing Templates
Give children tracing templates to draw with. If you don't have any on hand you can create some with cardboard or paper plates by cutting out simple pictures.

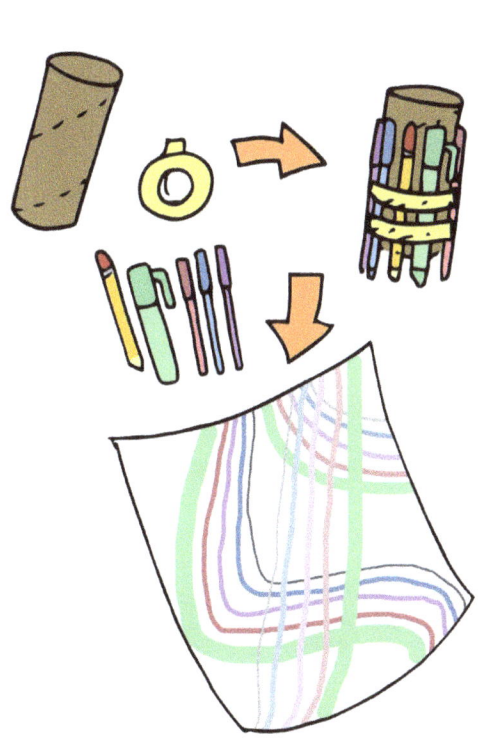

### Paper Roll Scribblers
Make a scribbler by taping various coloured pencils or textas onto the outside of a paper roll. Then hold it and draw patterns all over the paper.

# NOTES

# NOTES

Building activities provide great basic skills and should not be limited to 'boys play'. There are many learning attributes that come with building activities including counting, size, weight, volume, sorting, grouping, balance and gravity, spatial awareness, social and language skills, fine and gross motor development and hand eye coordination to name a few.

It is easy to incorporate STEAM (Science, Technology, Engineering, Art and Mathematics) within building activities. STEAM encourages innovative thinking, enhances problem-solving skills and helps in making connections to real-life in their learning.

Building also helps with creative aspects too as they are creating, designing, experimenting with trial and error, solving problems and learning about cause and effect. Children often learn patience, perseverance and how to deal with setbacks when it all comes tumbling down.

Building can also be a great activity to develop social skills as it takes cooperation, teamwork, turn-taking and discussions to design and create a construction together.

# Building

"I think I can. I know I can."

Watty Piper

## All Ages

**Alphabet Blocks**
Get children to count them as they stack them. They can try and create words or put them in alphabetical order.

**Velcro Blocks**
Add Velcro to a block set and see the creations they come up with.

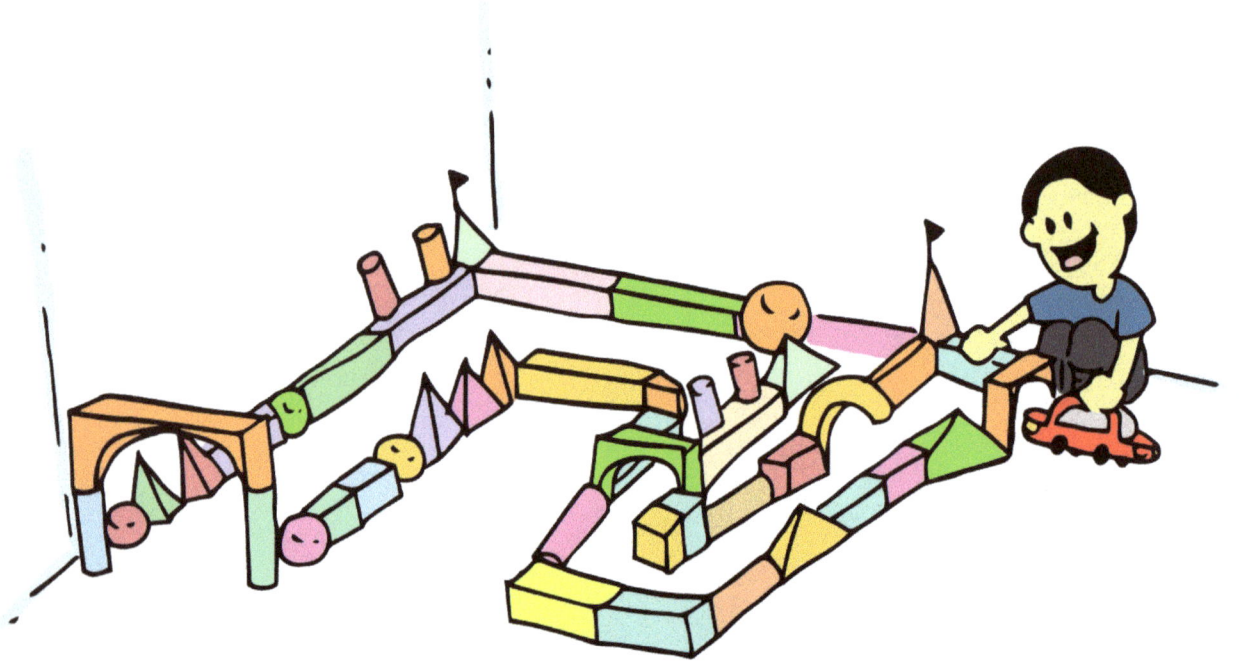

**Block Maze**
Show the children how we can use the blocks to create walls for a maze. They can then use cars, balls, figurines etc to try and get through the maze.

Early Childhood Edition

BUILDING

**Stacking Objects**
Stack like and unlike objects and try and get them to balance. You could use blocks, rocks, dice, containers, pom poms, glue sticks or combine rocks and dice or blocks and rocks etc.

**Block Recreation**
Take photos of block building creations and get children to recreate it by matching the blocks to those in the picture.

**Duplo or Lego**
Give them paper to either draw their design they want to make or sketch the creation they have made with the Lego.

Add in plastic animals, people or cars to extend their creativity.

**Wooden Blocks**
Incorporate different themed objects when the wooden blocks are out to extend their interests. Add in plastic animals to create a zoo or farm, stuffed animals to build larger cages or pens, cars to create roads and ramps, dolls to create beds and rooms. The possibilities are endless.

BUILDING

Teacher for a Day

**Race Tracks**
Give children cars with cardboard boxes, blocks, books, tape and any other material to help build ramps, jumps and tracks to improvise a race track.

**Train Tracks**
Let children build a track and add in cardboard boxes, paper and recycled art rubbish so they can make elevated tracks, tunnels out of curved paper, buildings etc.

**Foamy Foam Blocks**
Add shaving foam to small foam blocks to build towers. You can give them plastic knives or spoons to spread the foam on. As a variation you could add clay, play dough or blu-tac to wooden blocks to add a different dimension to building a tower.

**Building a River**
Children can build their own river using sand and water either in a container or in the sandpit. They can dig a path for the river in the sand then lay down some aluminium foil to stop the water absorbing into the sand. Add in rocks, sticks and leaves to create a dam, bridges or boats for the river.

**Stick Structures**
Using uncooked spaghetti, skewers, popsticks or toothpicks along with play dough, clay or blu-tac, get children to break off small pieces and roll into balls. Then they can build constructions by connecting the sticks and dough together.

# NOTES

# NOTES

Children are born to learn, wonder, explore and discover through play and Science is the perfect way to facilitate that. Science should be a natural extension on their learning and if presented right will aid in children's love of learning. Science in the Early Years should spark curiosity, develop problem solving skills and be lots of fun.

With a growing interest in STEAM education, it is important that as an Early Educator we make sure children have a positive attitude and enthusiasm towards Science.

There are some amazing science activities out there that can create unforgettable experiences for these young minds. Be sure to ask questions out loud to yourself and to them, model curiosity at the world around us, observe how and why things are the way they are. Ask them lots of "why" questions to help develop their critical thinking skills. Let them solve the problems themselves. Spark an interest in their inquisitive minds and they will be on their way to becoming lifelong learners.

# Science

"Science is a way of thinking much more than it is a body of knowledge."

**Carl Sagan**

## All Ages

Most of these activities can be adapted for all ages. They will be more teacher directed for the younger years and more interactive for the older ages.

### Cornflour Slime

Pour cornflour into a container and slowly add in water. Mix it carefully together adding more water until it becomes easy to stir. Stir it slowly then quickly. *Which is harder?* Quickly punch the slime then try placing your hand slowly into the mixture. *What happened?* Pick up the mixture and roll it into a ball. *What happens if you stop rolling it?*

**WHY?**

This is because unlike normal fluids that flow (like water, juice, milk) when you apply pressure to this mixture it acts like a solid (floor, chair, shoe).

**NOTE**

Dispose of the slime in the bin not the sink so it doesn't clog it!!

### Sink and Float

Discuss and demonstrate how some objects sink and some will float. Use a large water trough or tub (preferably see through) and put objects in one at a time. Get children to predict which objects would sink and which would float. Place them into a "Sink" and "Float" container once you have the results. For the older children you can write the predictions in a T-Chart then tick or cross them once you've found the outcomes.

| Sink | Float |
|---|---|
| Peg | Paper |
| Block | Toy boat |
| Crayon | Container |
| Scissors | Leaf |

**WHY?**

- Objects that are light for their size will float and objects that are heavy for their size will sink.

- The type of material it is made of can determine whether it will float or not, not just its weight (think of a paperclip).

- Things that contain air will float such as a blown-up balloon or a boat shaped item. You can trial this with a piece of play dough rolled in a ball or moulded into a boat shape.

Early Childhood Edition

**Vinegar Volcano**
Always a favourite. Put baking soda inside a drink bottle (you can add red colouring for effect). Bury the bottle in the sand to create a volcano. Pour vinegar into the bottle until the reaction of the ingredients causes it to explode out the top of the bottle like a volcano.

 **WHY?**
The chemical reaction between the vinegar (an acid) and the baking soda (a base) turns it into a new substance, a gas called carbon dioxide. When a base and an acid mix it causes an unstable reaction which causes it to fizz and explode as it is trying to escape.

**Self-inflating Balloon**
Get a clear drink bottle and put 4 tablespoons of vinegar in it. Using a funnel add 1 tablespoon of baking soda inside a balloon. Place the opening of the balloon over the bottle neck, minding not to spill any baking soda in yet. Once the balloon is on, let the baking soda fall into the vinegar and watch the balloon blow up all by itself when the two ingredients react with each other!

 **WHY?**
The chemical reaction between the vinegar (an acid) and the baking soda (a base) turns it into a new substance, a gas called carbon dioxide. The gas is trying to escape but since the bottle is sealed it has nowhere else to go so as it is pushing against the balloon it is inflating. Similarly we also breathe out carbon dioxide which is how we blow up balloons!

Teacher for a Day

**Flying Paper Planes**

As a group you are going to make 3 different designs of a paper plane. You will then test the planes to see which design flies the furthest. Record your findings in a chart and test it 3 times to make sure the results are conclusive.

## ? WHY?

When we do a science investigation we need to do a fair test. In order to do this we need to **Change** one thing (the plane design), **Measure** something (the distance it flies) and keep everything else the **Same** (where we throw it and how hard it is being thrown). Discuss how if we change too many variables, such as someone throwing their plane outside in the wind or one person throwing their plane off a chair, how it wouldn't make the test fair. The plane being thrown in the wind might blow it the wrong way or the person on the chair might have an advantage being a bit higher than the others. Discuss these possibilities and others and why it is important to keep all other variables the same.

**Scented Painting**

Add scented oils to paints and see if they can guess them. You could also show them the scented items and see if they can match them. Add lavender scent to purple, mint to green, citrus to orange, banana to yellow, strawberry to red, vanilla to beige, chocolate to brown etc.

## ? WHY?

Using their sense of smell makes this activity a sensory experience. Get them to guess the smell of the paint. They could match items to the paint. To make it more challenging, add the scents to colours not typically matching their smells.

**Colourful Absorption**

To teach the children the concept of absorption, place white flowers or celery sticks into different jars filled with coloured water. Draw predictions then monitor and record the findings by drawing the changes they observe each day. Did anything change with the flowers/celery? How long did it take to change colours? Which colours worked the best?

 **WHY?**

Plants have small tubes that carry water up through it to help it grow. Because the water is a different colour the colour also travels through the stems to the top of the plant changing the colours of the petals.

**Growing Seedlings**

Add soil half way up a clear plastic cup (so you can see the roots growing). Plant some seeds in the cup and water them regularly. Choose quick sprouting seeds such as radish, sunflower, cress, beans or alfalfa to see results faster. Get them to make observations of their plant like how long it took to show roots, how long it took to sprout. They could then measure its growth by putting marks on a popstick or using a ruler.

 **WHY?**

Discuss that a plant needs water, soil and sunlight to grow. You could show this by having seeds deprived of these things and observe what happens. Have one seed that gets no water, one no soil and one no sunlight (make sure they still have the other two components to grow). What happened to those seeds?

Teacher for a Day

**Musical Straw**
Flatten one end of the straw then cut the end of a straw into a point. Blow into it and it should make a funny sound. Cut the straw in different lengths and see if it makes different sounds.

## WHY?
The pointed end of the straw makes these funny sounds because of the fast vibrations between the ends. You can even feel it when you blow.

**Floating Egg**
Fill up a glass of water ¾ of the way and get children to predict what they think will happen to a raw egg if you place it in the glass. Discuss your observations. Next get children to help you add in 5 tablespoons of salt to a cup of water. Predict what will happen then place the egg in the cup and watch how it floats.

## WHY?
This is because salt water is denser than normal water. The egg sinks in the cup with normal water but floats in the cup with salty water. This is also why we can float much easier in salty water.

Early Childhood Edition

**Static Electricity**
You can explore static electricity through a variety of simple experiments.

Rub a blown-up balloon on your hair. What happens to your hair?

Rub a balloon on a woollen jumper or blanket then see if it sticks to the wall.

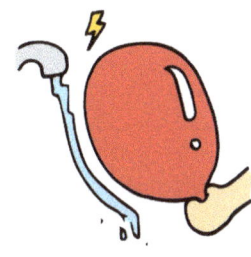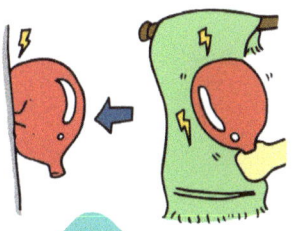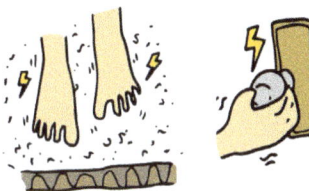

Rub a balloon on your head to charge it then put it near a running tap. What does the water do?

Shuffle your feet across carpet then touch something metal and see if you get a "shock".

 **WHY?**

Electricity is a type of energy. Static electricity happens when you rub two things together. This electric charge works like a magnet making things pull closer and stick (balloon stuck to the wall) or go further away (hair standing up or water bending away).

---

**Tie-dye Surface Tension**
Put a thin layer of milk in a dish or plate then add in a few drops of food colouring spaced around the dish. Get a cotton tip and dip it into dishwashing detergent. Put the cotton tip in the middle of the food colouring and watch the milk and colours swirl around.

 **WHY?**

The surface of a liquid is like a 'skin' which is called surface tension. When the skin or surface tension is broken by the detergent, the food colouring and milk swirl around together making interesting patterns on the broken surface. You can keep repeating this by re-dipping the cotton tip in the detergent. Be careful not to stir the mixture.

# NOTES

# NOTES

Fine motor means "small muscles". Developing these skills in children is refining their individual ability to manoeuver the muscles in their fingers, thumbs and hands. It is an important skill to aid in tasks such as feeding, writing, cutting, doing up buttons and zips, tying shoelaces and many other self-help tasks.

Children's hands need to build up strength in order to do many everyday duties and we can help develop this through fun activities and play.

# Fine Motor Skills

"Do what you can, with what you have, where you are."

Theodore Roosevelt

Teacher for a Day

## 0-2 years

**FINE MOTOR SKILLS**

**Droppers**
Get a container with water and have the children practise squeezing the dropper to suck up and release the water.

**Shake It**
Give the children keys, rattles or shakers to grab and shake around.

**Play Dough**
Play dough has many benefits for developing fine motor skills. Check out page 156 for detailed activities.

**Finger Plays and Rhymes**
Do finger plays to the children and encourage them to do it back. Round and Round the Garden, Two Little Dicky Birds, Where is Thumbkin etc.

**Texture Play**
Using containers or tubs put in different textured material for them to play with e.g. cooked or uncooked pasta, rice, shaving foam. You could also add hidden objects to find.

**Nature Play**
Give children sticks, twigs, rocks, bark, flowers, leaves and shells to play with. They could then do a collage with them, sort them, press them in dough or bury them in sand.

**Scrunching Paper**
Give children newspaper, brochures or magazines to tear and scrunch into balls. You could then practise throwing the paper balls to work on their gross motor skills.

**Cars**
Put out different sized cars for them to play with including smaller cars. You could make a track on the carpet with tape or blocks, put them in play dough or sand for them to drive them through.

**Drawing**
Using different writing materials to draw with is a great way to work on their fine motor and pre writing skills. Small, broken and stubby crayons are often thrown away but are particularly good for developing this skill.

Early Childhood Edition

## 0-2 years

### Pom Pom Push
Using a small box or egg carton, cut out small holes, big enough so that a pom pom can be pushed through it. Colour around the rim of the hole and then get the children to push the pom poms through the holes.

*Extension*
*Get them to match the coloured pom pom with the right coloured hole.*

### Feely Board or Boxes
Using different textured material you can make a board or tape it to a table. Material to use could be sandpaper, bubblewrap, carpet cut off, lino cut out etc.

You could also make feely boxes by cutting out holes in a shoebox and putting random objects inside it for them to touch and grab at.

### Cooking
Using cooking utensils is a great natural way to encourage fine motor skills. You could make play dough or do a cooking lesson with the group or set up a play kitchen with spoons, forks, spatulas, whisks along with cups and bowls for them to mix, stir and pour with.

### Stick Threading
Get a kebab stick that is placed in play dough to stand on its own or a pipe cleaner. Next get children to thread different objects onto it. You could use pasta, fruit loops, beads, small hair ties, patty pans with holes cut in them or anything you can find with a hole in it!

**FINE MOTOR SKILLS**

Teacher for a Day

## 3-6 years

**FINE MOTOR SKILLS**

**Feely Bags**
Put random items into a bag and get children to touch, feel and grab to guess what it is. Older children can match their findings to a clue card and cross off their findings.

**Dress Ups**
Provide dress up clothes with different fasteners such as buttons, zips, press studs, buckles etc.

**Grab It**
Pick up cotton balls, pom poms, shells, rocks or gems using tweezers/tongs or pegs. Hide these items in foam, rice or cooked spaghetti etc. for an added element.

**Box Collage**
Give children access to craft with scissors, sticky tape and colours and go crazy!

**Magnets**
Magnets can be used to explore how they attract and resist as well as move metal objects around.

**Carpentry**
Using nails, hammers and wood get the children "working" on their hand skills.

**Lego**
Lego is great for getting those fingers working and developing the fine motor skills.

**Messy Play**
Water, slime, wet sand, shaving foam, goop, and clay are all a fun way to explore with their fingers and hands.

**Tracing**
Give students a black lined colouring in picture and some tracing paper or baking paper and get them to copy the picture underneath.

**Washing Babies**
Give children baby dolls, baths, towels, clothes, a clothesline and pegs and let them play and develop their fine motor skills in a real world setting.

**Tactile Picture**
Place buttons/tokens/pasta on to a patterned picture e.g. ladybug or leopard spots, rays of a sun using pasta, a caterpillar's body using buttons.

**Play Dough**
Play dough has many benefits for developing fine motor skills. Children can hide small objects such as marbles in them.

Check out page 156 for more detailed activities.

*Early Childhood Edition*

**3-6 years**

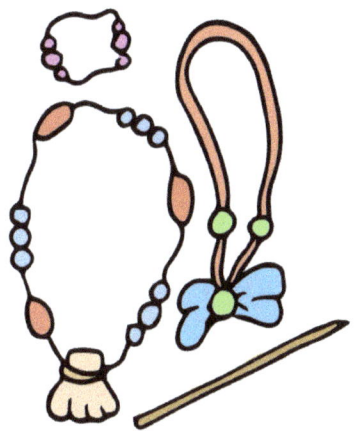

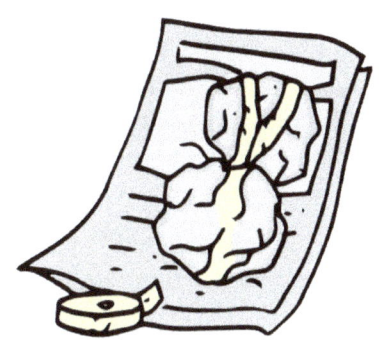

### Threading
Using string, wool, pipe cleaners, a stick or kebab stick, get children to practise their threading. You could use pasta, fruit loops, beads, small hair ties, cut up straws, paper with holes punched in them or anything you can find with a hole in it! Necklaces and bracelets are always a hit with this activity.

### Drawing
Using different writing materials to draw with is a great way to work on their fine motor and pre writing skills. Small, broken and stubby crayons are often thrown away but are particularly good for developing this skill.

### Paper Ball Toss
Give the children newspaper, magazine or brochures to scrunch into balls. They can then use tape to wrap around and secure it into a ball. Using the ball they can play a game by shooting it into a basket or container.

**FINE MOTOR SKILLS**

### Cutting
Cutting with scissors is an important skill to develop and requires strength in their fingers and hands. Any cutting activities will help with this.

*Some ideas are-*
- Cutting up pictures from magazines or brochures and sticking them on paper. They can create a birthday or Christmas shopping list or decorate a card for someone with pictures they might like.
- Cutting play dough with scissors. Practise rolling it into a snake then cutting it.
- Cutting around a given shape or along a line. Draw a straight, wavy, zigzag line for them to cut along.
- Cut up cooked spaghetti.
- Cut up craft items for collage such as wool, feathers, patty pans, ribbon etc.
- Cut the grass or trim a bush.

# PLAY DOUGH

Play dough is a staple item for the Early Years. It enhances fine motor skill development by strengthening muscle tone in their hands and fingers and helps with hand-eye coordination. It is great for creativity with endless opportunities for making and designing unique creations. Play dough helps encourage social skills when used with small groups and can be a great calming and therapeutic tool. It can also be a great way to teach Literacy and Numeracy. There are endless things to do with Play dough.

## Play Dough Recipe

| 2 cups of Plain Flour | 2 tablespoons of Vegetable Oil | ½ cup of Salt | 2 tablespoons of Cream of Tartar | Up to 1 ½ L of boiling water (adding a bit at a time until it feels right.) | Food colouring |

Mix all of the ingredients together, slowly adding in the water till you reach the right texture. You can make different colours, scents or add in glitter to change it up.

## Things to put the play dough on

 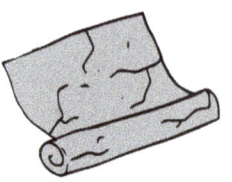 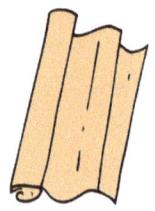  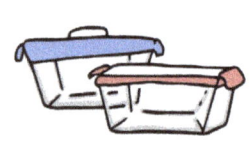

Wipeable table top | Aluminum foil | Baking paper | Cardboard boxes large or small | Large container

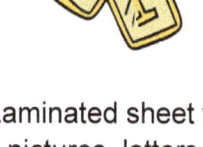   

Laminated sheet with pictures, letters or numbers to copy | Laminated placemats | Laminated table cloth | Water trough

Early Childhood Edition

## Things to add with play dough

 Matchsticks
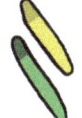 Paddlepop sticks
 Rocks, leaves, flowers and twigs
 Sea Shells
 Candles and patty pans
 Keys

 Sequins, pipe cleaners, ribbon, buttons, google eyes, pom poms
 Small containers
 Toy soldiers or figurines
 Plastic dinosaurs, animals and insects
 Play food
 Alphabet magnets

 Wooden blocks
 Toy cars and trucks
 Dry pasta or dried beans
 Fake flowers
 String or wool

## Tools to use with play dough

 Play dough tools - cutters, rolling pin, scissors, etc.
 Tools - nuts, bolts, hammers and screwdrivers
 Cookie cutters
 Ice tray
 Potato Masher
 Scissors

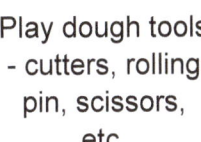 Plastic knives, forks, spoons
 Child-friendly pizza cutters
 Ice-cream scoop
 Garlic press
 Cake and cupcake tins

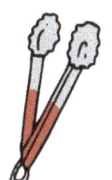 Tongs
 Melon baller
 Food moulds and shapes
 Bowls, plates, cups
 Combs

# NOTES

# NOTES

Gross motor is the physical skills we all need in order to crawl, stand, sit, walk, run, hop, skip, jump, ride, swim, catch, throw, kick and all of the other active movements in our daily lives. This is an imperative skill to learn in order to play actively with friends (by climbing in a playground), participate in sports (by kicking, catching and throwing) and for self-help skills (by being able to stand on one leg while putting pants on).

Crossing midline is also an important skill to develop. This action is where children are able to cross over their body to perform a task such as reaching for something with their right hand when it on the left side of their body or sitting cross-legged on the floor. Crossing the body's midline helps in many everyday tasks such as writing, getting dressed and playing sport and can impact a child's development and learning.

Gross motor skills can affect balance and movement as it involves using the core stabilising muscles. Children need to work on their muscular strength and endurance, timing and control, body awareness and coordination, crossing midline and muscle tone.

Teacher for a Day

**All Ages**

# Skills to Practise

walking forwards and backwards, quickly and slowly, big steps and small steps

jumping with two feet together

jumping off something and landing

hopping on one foot at a time

tip-toeing

balancing on one foot

balancing and walking along a beam

running on the spot, fast, slow, forwards and backwards

crawling on knees or on hands and feet either face down or with back towards the ground

climbing up and over frames

side-stepping by walking then progress to running

skipping (without a rope)

leaping and frog jumps

swinging and hanging on a bar

rolling like a log or forward rolls (be very careful doing these)

star jumps

pedalling a bike

balancing on a balance bike (if you have them)

Early Childhood Edition

**Obstacle Course**
You can set one up inside or outside and use climbing frames, slides, tunnels, hoops, stepping blocks, balls, skipping ropes and anything else that will get their bodies moving.

You can even do it with no equipment by drawing in chalk on the ground the movements you would like them to do.

All Ages

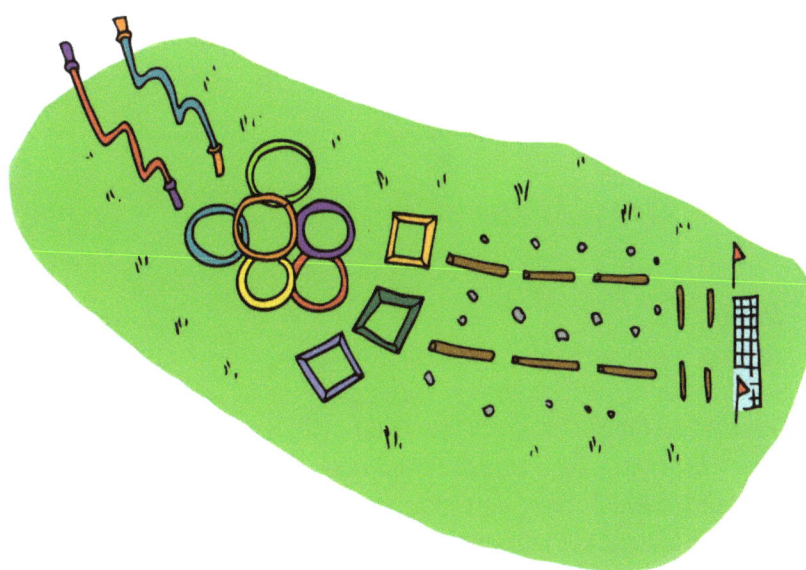

*Walk, jump, hop, crawl or sidestep on the straight, wavy or zigzag line. Do 5 star jumps in the circle. Jump like a frog from the triangle to the square. At each number jump that many times. Skip around and around the spiral. Jump over the lines on the ground.*

**Skipping Rope**
A skipping rope can be using in the traditional way, but it is a tricky skill to master for the young ones. Some other ways to use it is-

To spin it slow and low around in circles and get the children to jump over it.

Wobble the rope like a snake in the grass and get children to jump over it.

Hold it up at both ends and play limbo with it.

Two people hold it at each end and swing it around and the children need to run through without getting hit. The more advanced can try jumping on their way through.

Place it on the ground in different shapes and get children to balance on it like a tight rope.

Tie two ropes together and two people hold the ropes with their legs (like the game Elastics). Students can then practise jumping over and between the rope. Move the rope higher up the legs for more of a challenge.

**GROSS MOTOR SKILLS**

Teacher for a Day

### Yoga
Yoga is a great skill for stretching, calming and promoting mindfulness. Practise Downward Dog, Cat and Cow Pose, Child's Pose, Standing Tree Pose, Star Pose, Warrior Pose, Cobra (with tongue out) etc. Improvise a rocket launching into space, the sun rising, butterflies opening their wings and trees swaying side to side.

### Climbing
Climbing frames and ladders are the best and safest way for children to practise this skill. Ensure that they are safely positioned and that they are changed regularly to encourage an interest in the activity.

### Ball Skills
Catching, throwing, kicking and bouncing are very important skills to practise.
You can do this by throwing with balls, small bean bags, stuffed toys or any other soft object.

**Variations to practise**

- Dribbling a bouncy ball by hitting it repeatedly
- Kicking a ball from the ground then progressing to kicking it from your hands
- Throwing and catching with someone else
- Bouncing the ball and catching it
- Kicking or throwing a ball to a wall. You could make a target on the wall for more of a challenge
- Throwing the ball up in the air to themselves and catching it
- Throwing a beanbag, ball or soft object to a target e.g. in a hoop on the ground, through a basketball hoop, into a bucket etc.
- Kicking, catching and chasing the ball with someone else

### Hop, Skip and Jump Hopstoch

Hopscotch is a great, simple game to teach hopping, skipping, jumping and tossing skills. Draw up a hopscotch court from 1-10. Children use a beanbag, pebble, coin, etc. and throw it onto a number which means that square must be skipped. The children must hop and jump through the court to the end.

Not only does this game practise important gross motor skills but it also teaching turn-taking, lining up, patience and socialisation.

### Hoops

Hula hoops are a great tool for gross motor practise. Other than the usual hula-ing around the middle they can be used in a variety of ways such as-

- Spinning around arms, wrists, hands, legs, ankles and necks.
- Use them for a sorting or racing game where children need to run and collect items for their colours, shapes or description and return them to the hoops.
- Hold them or tie them up for children to crawl or jump through.
- Hold them or tie them up for children to throw things through.
- Place them on the ground for children to jump, hop and step through.
- Place them on the ground for children to aim and throw things into it. Older children can use point scoring cards to practise tallying too.

# NOTES

# NOTES

Free expression and creativity are just some of the benefits of Dramatic Play. These open-ended activities give children an opportunity to bust stereotypes by allowing them to choose freely what they want to wear and who they want to be, promoting confidence and freethinking.

It is in Home Corner where they will practise self-help skills by "making dinner", "pouring drinks", and dressing themselves. They learn compassion and helpfulness when they are caring for their "babies" and practise responsibility when they are going off to "work". It is through dramatic play that their language skills are enhanced as they role-play with friends and build stronger social bonds and connections with their peers.

# Dramatic Play

"Why fit in when you were born to stand out?"

Dr Suess

Teacher for a Day

## 3-6 years

**Clusters**
Give students an instruction (walk backwards, crawl, hop, tiptoe, stomp, jump, etc.), call out a number and the students need to get into groups of this amount. It is a good way to get students into groups for a follow-up activity.

## Bean Game

  Students do the actions of each bean when the teacher calls them out. Choose some or all of these.

| | | | |
|---|---|---|---|
| Jelly bean | wobbling | Butter Bean | slide around on your bottom |
| Jumping bean | jump on the spot | Full of Beans | dance around energetically |
| Runner bean | run on the spot | Coffee bean | cough madly |
| Chilli bean | shiver and shake | Tinned beans | get into small groups |
| Frozen bean | freeze | Bean Casserole | students all join hands |
| Broad bean | giant steps around the room | Beanstalk | crouch down and grow up to the sky |
| Baked bean | sunbake on the floor | Magic Bean | wave a wand |
| String bean | arms straight up in the air as thin as string | Bean bag | one student sits on the floor and a partner sits on their lap |

# Minute Mime

A child is chosen to act out a word given and then the group need to guess what it is.

| | |
|---|---|
| Snake | Tiger |
| Running in a race | Playing soccer |
| Brushing your hair | Dog |
| Playing the guitar | Licking an ice cream |
| Plane flying | Frog |
| Karate | Having a drink |
| Brushing your teeth | Tying your shoelace |
| Getting dressed | Giving a hug |
| Digging a hole | Painting a Picture |

**Animal Walk**
Get children to walk around the space as an animal that you call out.

For example: kangaroo- hopping, frog- leaping, tiger- prowling, snake- slithering, cheetah- running etc.

**Intro and Applause**
Children walk in the circle or to the front of the class one at a time. They introduce themselves and tell the class one interesting fact about themselves. The audience then applauses and they stay standing up until the applause ends.

Teacher for a Day

## All Ages

**Dress Ups**
Provide different dress ups such as preloved superhero costumes, princes dresses, emergency service uniforms, tutus, high heels, jackets, hats, gloves, scarves and any other clothing you have access to. Watch their imaginations run wild as they roleplay different characters and scenarios.

**Puppets**
Give children hand or finger puppets to create their own show. Model a show or story to start with to give them an idea of what they can do with the puppets.

**Fairy Tale Plays**
Introduce the class to a Fairy Tale and get them to re-enact it. Set up the scene and add in costumes if possible. Children that learn the lines well exhibit great listening and comprehension skills.

**Play Shops**
Set up a shop whether it is a supermarket, ice cream parlour, pizza shop or pet shop. Explain that there needs to be a shopkeeper and customers and let them take turns to role play.

**Doctors**
Set up a hospital or doctors surgery with beds, bandages, doctors equipment, syringes, whiteboards and notepads. Encourage them to role play doctors, nurses, patients and visitors.

Early Childhood Edition

### Restaurant
Set up a restaurant with table settings, play food, plates and cutlery, and notepads. Discuss what will be the name of the restaurant and what will be on the menu then write and draw up the food for the customers to choose from.

### Offices
Provide keyboards, phones, paper on clipboards with pens and desks so the children can roleplay being at "work".

### Beauty Salon
Put in bottles of shampoo, old perfume and moisturiser bottles, combs, spray bottles and set up chairs and mirrors to create a beauty salon.

### Post Office
Set up mail boxes and give the children cards, postcards, boxes, tape and writing material to create their own post office experience.

### Archaeologist
Fill a water trough with sand and bury dinosaurs, shells and rocks in it. Give the children paint brushes, sticks and spades to explore and become the archaeologists.

### Pets
Set up a scene to suit pet dogs or cats with a bed, bowl for eating and drinking and leashes along with other stuffed animals if their interests are swinging this way.

**DRAMATIC PLAY**

# NOTES

# NOTES

Early Childhood Edition

The benefits of music in Early Years Education spans much further than learning how to sing nursery rhymes. Music is a language and it helps develop the whole child in a variety of ways. Music aids in accelerating brain development, enhancing literacy and language skills, increases vocabulary, improves social and emotional skills, and gives children skills to help them prepare for school.

Not only does music have many benefits, it also brings happiness and joy to a child. Young babies find music soothing, toddlers love listening to nursery rhymes, the bigger kids enjoy singing and acting along to action songs and everyone loves having a dance to some fun music.

Be sure to incorporate music into your day through singing, listening to music from different genres, playing instruments or finding rhythm and beat using your body or things around you.

# ♪ Music

"A child who sings is a happy child."

**Elder Enrique Falabella**

Teacher for a Day

## 0-2 years

**Musical Freeze**
Play music and children need to freeze when the music stops.

### Five Little Ducks
Five little ducks
Went out one day
Over the hills and far away
Mother duck said
"Quack, quack, quack, quack"
But only four little ducks came back.

(Repeat)
But only three little ducks came back.
(Repeat)
But only two little ducks came back.

One little duck
Went out one day
Over the hills and far away
Mother duck said
"Quack, quack, quack, quack."
But none of the five little ducks came back.

Sad mother duck
Went out one day
Over the hills and far away
The sad mother duck said
"Quack, quack, quack."
And all of the five little ducks came back.

### Rain Rain Go Away
Rain, rain go away
Come again another day.
Rain, rain go away
Little Johnny wants to play.

### Head, Shoulders, Knees and Toes
Head, shoulders, knees and toes
Knees and toes
(Repeat)
And eyes and ears and mouth and nose
Head, shoulders, knees and toes
Knees and toes

### Five Little Monkeys
Five little monkeys jumping on the bed
One fell off and bumped his head
Mama called the doctor and the doctor said:
"No more monkeys jumping on the bed!"

(Repeat)
Four…
Three…
Two…
One…

Now there's no little monkeys jumping on the bed.
They're all jumping on the sofa instead!

### Five Little Speckled Frogs

Five little speckled frogs
Sat on a speckled log
Eating some most delicious grubs - yum, yum
One jumped into the pool
Where it was nice and cool
Now there are four green speckled frogs - glub, glub.

(Repeat)
Four…
Three…
Two…
One…
Now there are no green speckled frogs - glub, glub.

### Old MacDonald Had a Farm

Old McDonald had a farm, E-I-E-I-O
And on his farm he had a cow, E-I-E-I-O
With a "moo-moo" here and a "moo-moo" there
Here a "moo" there a "moo"
Everywhere a "moo-moo"
Old McDonald had a farm, E-I-E-I-O

(Repeat)
And on his farm he had a duck/ horse/ sheep/ dog, E-I-E-I-O

### Where Is Thumbkin?

Where is Thumbkin?
Where is Thumbkin?
Here I am!
Here I am!
How are you today, Sir?
Very well. I thank you!
Run away
Run away.

(Repeat)

Where is Pointer?
Where is Tall boy?
Where is Ringo?
Where is Pinky?

### One Two Buckle My Shoe

One, two
Buckle my shoe,
Three, four
Open the door,
Five, six
Pick up sticks,
Seven, eight
Lay them straight,
Nine, ten
A good fat hen.

Teacher for a Day

### Miss Polly Had a Dolly
Miss Polly had a dolly who was sick, sick, sick.
So she phoned for the doctor
to come quick, quick, quick.
The doctor came with his bag and his hat,
And knocked at the door with a rat-a-tat-tat.

He looked at the dolly and shook his head,
And said "Miss Polly put her straight to bed.
He wrote a paper for a pill, pill, pill.
I'll be back in the morning with the bill, bill, bill.

### Little Peter Rabbit
Little Peter Rabbit had a fly upon his nose,
Little Peter Rabbit had a fly upon his nose,
Little Peter Rabbit had a fly upon his nose,
And he flipped it and he flapped it and it flew away.

### This Little Piggy
This little piggy went to market
This little piggy stayed at home
This little piggy had roast beef
This little piggy had none
And this little piggy went
"Wee, Wee, Wee" all the way home!

### Rock-a-Bye Baby
Rock-a-bye baby, on the treetop
When the wind blows, the cradle will rock
When the bough breaks, the cradle will fall
And down will come baby, cradle and all

### If You're Happy And You Know It
If you're happy and you know it,
clap your hands.
If you're happy and you know it,
clap your hands.
If you're happy and you know it,
And you really want to show it,
(or then your face will surely show it)
If you're happy and you know it,
clap your hands.

Then you can go on with i.e.:

If you're happy and you know it,
tap your toe/nod your head/
blink your eyes...

Or experiment with emotions
with these variations-
If you're excited and you know it,
shout "Hooray!"...
If you're angry and you know it,
stomp your feet...
If you're sad and you know it,
have a cry...
If you're loving and you know it,
blow a kiss...

### The Wheels On The Bus
The wheels on the bus go
round and round,
Round and round
Round and round.
The wheels on the bus go
round and round,
all day long.

The horn on the bus goes
Beep, beep, beep
The wipers on the bus go
Swish, swish, swish
The baby on the bus says
"Wah, wah, wah"
The mummy on the bus says
"Shush, shush, shush"
The daddy on the bus goes
"Read, read, read"
The bell on the bus goes
"Ding, ding, ding"
The Driver on the bus says
"Move on back"
The people on the bus laugh
"Ha-ha-ha"

### Row Row Row Your Boat
Row, row, row your boat,
Gently down the stream.
Merrily, merrily, merrily, merrily
Life is but a dream.

Variations-

Row, row, row your boat,
Gently down the stream.
If you see a crocodile
Don't forget to scream!

Rock, rock, rock your boat,
Gently down the river
If you see a Polar bear
Don't forget to shiver!

### One Two Three Four Five
One, two, three, four, five,
Once I caught a fish alive,
six, seven, eight, nine, ten,
Then I let it go again.

Why did you let it go?
Because it bit my finger so.
Which finger did it bite?
This little finger on the right.

### Ring-a-rosie
Ring-a-ring-o-rosie
A pocket full of posies
A tissue! A tissue!
We all fall down!

The cows are in the meadow
Eating buttercups!
A tissue! A tissue!
We all jump up!

### Round and Round The Garden
Round and round the garden
Like a teddy bear
One step, two step
Tickle you under there!

### Twinkle Twinkle Little Star
Twinkle, twinkle, little star,
How I wonder what you are.
Up above the world so high,
Like a diamond in the sky.

Twinkle, twinkle, little star,
How I wonder what you are!

### Teddy Bear, Teddy Bear
Teddy bear, teddy bear,
Turn around!
Teddy bear, teddy bear,
Touch the ground!
Teddy bear, teddy bear,
Jump up high!
Teddy bear, teddy bear,
Touch the sky!

Teddy bear, teddy bear,
Bend down low!
Teddy bear, teddy bear,
Touch you toes!
Teddy bear, teddy bear,
Turn out the light!
Teddy bear, teddy bear,
Say good night!

### See Saw Margery Daw
See Saw Margery Daw,
Johnny shall have
a new master,
Johnny shall earn
but a penny a day.
Because he can't work
any faster.

### Ten Little Fingers
Ten little fingers,
ten little toes,
Two little ears
and one little nose
Two little eyes
that shine so bright
And one little mouth
to kiss mother goodnight.

### I Hear Thunder (To the tune of "Where is Thumbkin")
I hear thunder!
I hear thunder!
Hark don't you,
hark don't you?
Pitter, patter raindrops,
Pitter patter raindrops,
I'm wet through
and so are you!

Teacher for a Day

**3-6 years**

### Musical Chairs

Chairs are set up so that there is one less chair than the amount of children playing. Music is playing and once the music stops, the children must find a chair to sit on. The child that misses out needs to sit out and the game continues until you have a winner. You can play this with small mats instead of chairs too.

### Found Sound

Students explore the room and find something they can use to make a sound. They will share their Found Sound and can vote on the most original sound.

### Storm Musical

Using body parts only, students are to create a storm musical. They will start with the pitter patter of rain drops, moving on to a light shower and progress to a heavy downpour. Choose some students to add in the howling wind and claps of thunder. Once they have reached the crescendo of the storm, get students to quiet down to the pitter patter and then stop.

### Doggy, Doggy Where's Your Bone?

Students sit in a large circle. The teacher chooses a student to be the 'doggy' and to close their eyes in the middle of the circle. The teacher gives an item (the bone) to one of the students sitting in the circle to hide behind their back.

The class sings "Doggy, doggy where's your bone, somebody stole it from your home. Guess who, maybe you? Wake up doggy, find your bone."

The 'doggy' in the middle of the circle gets 3 guesses at who is hiding the 'bone' behind their back.

### Who Stole the Cookie from the Cookie Jar?

Children sit in a circle and the teacher chooses a child to be in the middle. He or she must close their eyes while another child in the circle is chosen to have "the cookie" (this can be any object). All children then hide their hands behind their backs and the middle child opens their eyes to start guessing who has the cookie while singing with the group.

Class- "Who stole the cookie from the cookie jar?"
Child- "Cleo."
Class- "Cleo stole the cookie from the cookie jar."
Cleo- " Who me?"
Class- "Yes you!"
Cleo- "Couldn't be!"
Class- "Then who stole the cookie from the cookie jar?"

Continue on until you find the "thief" or they have taken enough guesses.

### Sound Patterns
Get children to repeat sound patterns that you make using clapping, clicking, knee slapping, stomping, tapping etc.

*Clap-clap-click-clap*
*Stomp-clap- stomp- stomp-clap*

### Soft and Loud
Get children to explore soft and loud noises. They could use instruments, voice and bodies or found objects to make soft sounds, loud sounds, medium sounds and no sound on the teacher's given cue.

Teacher for a Day

# ACTION SONGS

### Music Man
If possible use instruments to play this song otherwise just act it out choosing any instruments you like.

The Music Man:
"I am the music man,
I come from down the way,
and I can play!"
Audience:
"What can you play?"

The Music Man:
"I can play the piano!"
Sing "Pia-pia-pia-no, pia-no, pia-no; pia-pia-pia-no, pia-pia-no" to the tune.

Actions - act out playing chords on a piano

Trombone:
The Music Man:
"I play the trombone!"
Sing "oomp-pa-oomp-pa-ooomp-pa-paaaa, oomp-pa-paaaa, oomp-pa-paaa; oomp-pa-oomp-pa-oomp-pa-paaaa, oomp-pa-oomp-pa-pa" to the tune.

Actions - mime playing trombone.

### Wind The Bobbin Up
Wind the bobbin up,
Wind the bobbin up,
Pull, Pull, Clap, Clap, Clap,
Point to the ceiling
Point to the floor
Point to the window
Point to the door
Clap your hands together - 1, 2, 3,
Put your hands down on your knees.

### Bingo
There was a farmer
who had a dog,
And Bingo was his name-O.
B-I-N-G-O!
B-I-N-G-O!
B-I-N-G-O!
And Bingo was his name-O!

There was a farmer
who had a dog,
And Bingo was his name-O.
(Clap)-I-N-G-O!
(Clap)-I-N-G-O!
(Clap)-I-N-G-O!
And Bingo was his name-O!

(Repeat)
(Clap - Clap)-N-G-O!
(Clap - Clap - Clap)-G-O!
(Clap - Clap - Clap - Clap)-O!
(Clap - Clap - Clap - Clap - Clap)

### Hokey Pokey
You put your right foot in
You put your right foot out
You put your right foot in
And you shake it all about
You do the Hokey Pokey
and you turn yourself around
That's what it's all about!

(Repeat)

You put your left foot in
You put your right hand in
You put your left hand in
You put your head in
You put your whole self in

### I'm Taking Home my Baby Bumble Bee
I'm taking home my baby
bumble bee
Won't my mummy
be so proud of me
I'm taking home my baby
bumble bee
Ouch! It stung me!

I'm squishing up my baby
bumble bee
Won't my mummy
be so proud of me
I'm squishing up my baby
bumble bee
Eww! It's all yucky!

I'm wiping off my baby
bumble bee
Won't my mummy
be so proud of me
I'm wiping off my baby
bumble bee
All clean!

### Sleeping Bunnies
See the bunnies sleeping
till it's nearly noon
Shall we wake them
with a merry tune?
They're so still, are they ill?
Wake up little bunnies!
Hop little bunnies,
hop, hop, hop
Hop, hop, hop -
Hop, hop, hop
Hop little bunnies,
hop, hop, hop
Hop, hop, hop...

Repeat
Skip little bunnies,
skip, skip, skip
Jump little bunnies,
jump, jump, jump
Sleep little bunnies,
sleep, sleep, sleep

Early Childhood Edition

### Dingle Dangle Scarecrow
When all the cows
were sleeping
and the sun had gone to bed
Up jumped the scarecrow
and this is what he said
"I'm a dingle dangle scarecrow
with a flippy, floppy hat,
I can shake my hands like this
and shake my feet like that."

When all the hens
were roosting
and the moon behind a cloud,
Up jumped the scarecrow
and shouted very loud
"I'm a dingle dangle scarecrow
with a flippy, floppy hat,
I can shake my hands like this
and shake my feet like that."

### A Sailor Went To Sea
A sailor went to sea,
sea, sea
To see what he could see,
see, see
But all that he could see,
see, see
Was the bottom
of the deep blue sea, sea, sea!

A sailor went to knee,
knee, knee
To see what he could knee,
knee, knee
But all that he could knee,
knee, knee
Was the bottom of the deep
blue knee, knee, knee!
(Sea, sea, sea)

A sailor went to chop,
chop, chop
To see what he could chop,
chop, chop
But all that he could chop,
chop, chop
Was the bottom of the deep
blue chop, chop, chop!
(Sea, sea, sea)
(Knee, knee, knee)

### The Farmer In The Dell
The farmer in the dell
The farmer in the dell
Hi-ho, the derry-o
The farmer in the dell

The farmer takes a wife
The farmer takes a wife
Hi-ho, the derry-o
The farmer takes a wife

(Repeat)

The wife takes a child
The child takes a nurse
The nurse takes a cow
The cow takes a dog
The dog takes a cat
The cat takes a mouse
(or rat)
The mouse takes the cheese
The cheese stands alone

### I'm a Peanut
I'm a peanut small and round
(bang one fist into your open
palm repeatedly)
Lying on the cold hard ground
Everybody steps on me
I'm as cracked as a nut can be

I'm a nut (click, click)
In a rut (click, click)
I'm a nut (click, click)
In a rut (click, click)

One day a little girl came by
(bang one fist into your open
palm repeatedly)
She looked at me and winked
her eye (wink)
She said I'll have you for me
tea
I replied "No you won't eat me!"

(Repeat chorus)

### Brush Your Teeth
When you get up
in the morning
at a quarter to one
and you want to
have a little fun
You brush your teeth
ch ch ch ch ch ch,
ch ch ch ch ch ch...

When you wake up
in the morning
at a quarter to two
and you want
something to do
You brush your teeth
ch ch ch ch ch ch,
ch ch ch ch ch ch....

When you wake up
in the morning
at a quarter to three
and you wanna
flash your smile at me
You brush your teeth
ch ch ch ch ch ch,
ch ch ch ch ch ch....

When you wake up
in the morning
at a quarter to four
and you think you hear
a knock on the door
You brush your teeth
ch ch ch ch ch ch,
ch ch ch ch ch ch....

When you wake up
in the morning
at a quarter to five
and you just can't wait
to come alive
You brush your teeth
ch ch ch ch ch ch,
ch ch ch ch ch ch....

### This Old Man

This old man, he played one
He played knick-knack on my thumb
Knick-knack paddy whack
Give the dog the bone
This old man came rolling home.

This old man, he played two
He played knick-knack on my shoe
Knick-knack paddy whack
Give the dog the bone
This old man came rolling home.

This old man, he played three
He played knick-knack on my knee
Knick-knack paddy whack
Give the dog the bone
This old man came rolling home.

This old man, he played four
He played knick-knack on my door
Knick-knack paddy whack
Give the dog the bone
This old man came rolling home.

This old man, he played five
He played knick-knack on my hive
Knick-knack paddy whack
Give the dog the bone
This old man came rolling home.

This old man, he played six
He played knick-knack with some sticks
Knick-knack paddy whack
Give the dog the bone
This old man came rolling home.

This old man, he played seven
He played knick-knack up in Heaven
Knick-knack paddy whack
Give the dog the bone
This old man came rolling home.

This old man, he played eight
He played knick-knack on my gate
Knick-knack paddy whack
Give the dog the bone
This old man came rolling home.

This old man, he played nine
He played knick-knack on my spine
Knick-knack paddy whack
Give the dog the bone
This old man came rolling home.

This old man, he played ten
He played knick-knack once again
Knick-knack paddy whack
Give the dog the bone
This old man came rolling home.

Early Childhood Edition

# COUNTING SONGS

**Johnny Works with One Hammer**
*Johnny works with one hammer,
One hammer, one hammer,
Johnny works with one hammer,
Then he works with two.*
**(Hammer one fist lightly on leg)**

*(Repeat)
… Two hammers*
**(Hammer both fists on legs)**
*… Three hammers*
**(Hammer both fists on legs
and one foot on the floor)**
*… Four hammers*
**(Hammer both fists on legs
and both feet on the floor)**
*Johnny works with five hammers,
Five hammers, five hammers,
Johnny works with five hammers*
**(Hammer both fists on legs, both feet on floor, and nod head down and up)**
*Then he goes to sleep.*
**(Pretend to go to sleep)**

**Ten Green Bottles**
*Ten green bottles sitting on the wall,
Ten green bottles sitting on the wall,
And if one green bottle
should accidentally fall,
There will be nine green bottles
sitting on the wall.*

*Nine green bottles sitting on the wall,
Nine green bottles sitting on the wall,
And if one green bottle
should accidentally fall,
There will be eight green bottles
sitting on the wall.*

*Eight green bottles sitting on the wall…
Seven green bottles sitting on the wall…*

*One green bottle sitting on the wall,
One green bottle sitting on the wall,
And if this green bottle
should accidentally fall,
There will no green bottles
sitting on the wall.*

Teacher for a Day

### Ants Go Marching
The ants go marching
one by one.
Hoorah! Hoorah!
The ants go marching
one by one.
Hoorah! Hoorah!
The ants go marching
one by one;
The little one stops
 to suck his thumb,
And they all go
marching down
into the ground
To get out of the rain.
Boom, boom, boom, boom!

(Repeat)
Two by two…
The little one stops
to tie his shoe…
Three by three…
The little one stops
to climb a tree…
Four by four…
The little one stops
to shut the door…
Five by five…
The little one stops
to take a dive…
Six by six…
The little one stops
to pick up sticks…
Seven by seven…
The little one stops
to pray to heaven…
Eight by eight…
The little one stops
to roller skate…
Nine by nine…
The little one stops
to check the time…
Ten by ten…
The little one stops
to shout "THE END!"

### Here is the Beehive
Here is the beehive.
(hold up a closed fist)
Where are the bees?
Hiding away
where nobody sees.
(move other hand around fist)
Watch and you'll see them
come out of the hive
(bend head close to fist)
One, two, three, four, five.
(hold fingers up one at a time)
Bzzzzzzzz… all fly away!
(wave fingers)

### Ten Little Indians
One, little two,
little three, little Indians
Four, little five,
little six, little Indians,
Seven, little eight,
little nine, little Indians
Ten little Indian boys.

Ten, little nine,
little eight, little Indians
Seven, little six,
little five, little Indians
Four, little three,
little two, little Indians
One little Indian boy.

### One Little Finger
One little finger, one little finger,
one little finger
Tap, tap, tap
Point to the ceiling,
point to the floor
And lay them on your lap.

Two little fingers….
Three little fingers….

You can do this
for all ten fingers
or you can do it by counting
in twos using both hands.

*Early Childhood Edition*

# 🎵 NURSERY RHYMES

Nursery rhymes and action songs have stood the test of time and come with many benefits. They are relatable and entertaining to young children and they are short, so perfect for young attention spans. They often use rhyme and repetition, which aid with early reading skills, and they emphasise different patterns of sounds in words helping children to understand syllables and phonemes in words. Songs or stories with actions are extremely beneficial to young children as they help to build the

- listening and following directions
- fine and gross motor skills
- increases memory and recall
- hand eye coordination
- language and vocabulary skills
- basic concepts- (alphabet, colours, numbers, animals, sounds etc)
- imagination and creativity
- social skills and cooperation
- promotes self-confidence.

### Mary Had a Little Lamb
*Mary had a little lamb,  
little lamb, little lamb.  
Mary had a little lamb,  
its fleece was white as snow.  
And everywhere  
that Mary went,  
Mary went, Mary went,  
and everywhere that Mary went  
- the lamb was sure to go.*

### Baa Baa Black Sheep
*Baa, baa, black sheep  
Have you any wool?  
Yes sir, yes sir  
Three bags full.  
One for my master  
And one for the dame  
One for the little boy  
Who lives down the lane.*

### I'm a Little Teapot
*I'm a little teapot  
Short and stout  
Here is my handle  
Here is my spout  
When I get all steamed up  
Hear me shout  
Just tip me over  
and pour me out!*

### Little Bo Peep
*Little Bo Peep has  
lost her sheep  
And can't tell where  
to find them  
Leave them alone  
And they'll come home*

### Little Miss Muffet
*Little Miss Muffet sat  
on a tuffet  
Eating her curds and whey  
Along came a spider  
Who sat down beside her  
And frightened Miss Muffet  
away.*

### Little Jack Horner
*Little Jack Horner sat  
in the corner  
Eating his Christmas pie,  
He put in his thumb  
and pulled out a plum  
And said "What a  
good boy am I!"*

Teacher for a Day

### Humpty Dumpty

*Humpty Dumpty sat on a wall.
Humpty Dumpty had a great fall.
All the king's horses and all the King's men
Could not put Humpty together again.*

*Humpty Dumpty sat on a wall.
Humpty Dumpty had a great fall.
All the king's horses and all the King's men
Could not put Humpty together again.*

### Hey Diddle Diddle

*Hey diddle diddle, the cat and the fiddle
The cow jumped over the moon
The little dog laughed to see such fun
And the dish ran away with the spoon!*

*Hey diddle diddle, the cat and the fiddle
The cow jumped over the moon
The little dog laughed to see such fun
And the dish ran away with the spoon!*

### It's Raining, It's Pouring

*It's raining, it's pouring.
The old man is snoring.
He bumped his head and went to bed
And he couldn't get up in the morning.*

*It's raining, it's pouring.
The old man is snoring.
He bumped his head and went to bed
And he couldn't get up in the morning.*

### Pat-a-Cake

*Pat-a-cake, pat-a-cake, baker's man.
Bake me a cake as fast as you can,
Pat it and prick it and mark it with B,
And bake it in the oven for baby and me.*

*Patty cake, patty cake, baker's man.
Bake me a cake as fast as you can,
Pat it and prick it and mark it with B,
And bake it in the oven for baby and me.*

### The Grand Old Duke of York

*Oh, The grand old Duke of York,
He had ten thousand men.
He marched them up to the top of the hill,
And he marched them down again.*

*And when they were up, they were up,
And when they were down, they were down,
And when they were only half-way up.
They were neither up nor down.*

### Three Blind Mice

*Three blind mice, three blind mice,
See how they run, see how they run!*

*They all ran after the farmer's wife,
Who cut off their tails with a carving knife,*

*Did you ever see such a thing in your life,
As three blind mice?*

*Early Childhood Edition*

### Jack and Jill
Jack and Jill went up the hill
To fetch a pail of water.
Jack fell down
and broke his crown,
And Jill came tumbling after.

Up Jack got, and home did trot,
As fast as he could caper,
He went to bed
to mend his head
With vinegar and brown paper.

### Sing a Song of Sixpence
Sing a song of sixpence
- A pocket full of rye.
Four and twenty blackbirds
- Baked in a pie.

When the pie was opened,
The birds began to sing.
Wasn't that a dainty dish
To set before the king?

The king was in
his counting house,
Counting out his money.
The queen was in the parlour,
Eating bread and honey.

The maid was in the garden,
Hanging out the clothes.
When down came a blackbird
And pecked off her nose!

### Old Mother Hubbard
Old Mother Hubbard
Went to the cupboard
To give her poor dog a bone.
But when she got there
The cupboard was bare
And so the poor dog had none.

### Mary Mary Quite Contrary
Mary, Mary, quite contrary
How does your garden grow?
With silver bells,
And cockle shells,
And pretty maids all in a row.

Mary, Mary, quite contrary
How does your garden grow?
With silver bells,
And cockle shells,
And pretty maids all in a row.

### There Was a Crooked Man
There was a crooked man,
and he walked a crooked mile.
He found a crooked sixpence
upon a crooked stile.
He bought a crooked cat,
which caught a crooked mouse,
And they all lived together
in a little crooked house.

### Hot Cross Buns
Hot cross buns!
Hot cross buns!
One a penny, two a penny.
Hot cross buns!

If you have no daughters,
Give them to your sons!
One a penny, two a penny.
Hot cross buns!

### Polly Put The Kettle On
Polly put the kettle on
Polly put the kettle on
Polly put the kettle on
We will all have tea.

Sukey take it off again
Sukey take it off again
Sukey take it off again
They've all gone away.

### Incy Wincy Spider
The incy wincy spider
went up the water spout.
Down came the rain,
and washed the spider out.
Up came the sun,
and dried up all the rain,
and the incy wincy spider
went up the spout again.

### Hickory Dickory Dock
Hickory, dickory, dock
The mouse ran up the clock.
The clock struck one
The mouse ran down
Hickory, dickory, dock.

Hickory, dickory, dock
The mouse ran up the clock.
The clock struck two
And down he flew
Hickory, dickory, dock.

# NOTES

# NOTES

Early Childhood Edition

MUSIC

Games are a great way for children to build on social skills such as turn-taking, waiting patiently, giving and adhering to directions and understanding rules and consequences. Playing games teaches children cooperation, self-regulation and how to play fairly which are invaluable life skills. Not only do children learn an abundance of skills, they are having fun in doing so, making learning meaningful in their world.

While much of their play should be unstructured, it can be beneficial for children to learn and play more structured games. Often once they are familiar with a game you will find them instructing and teaching others on how to play it. These games often will hold a nostalgic memory in later days too.

# Games

"Minds are like parachutes-
they only function when open."

Thomas Dewar

Teacher for a Day

## 0-2 years

**Duck, Duck, Goose**
This old favourite is always a hit. Sitting in a circle somebody walks around the circle calling out "duck, duck, duck…" until they choose someone to be the "goose". The "goose" then tries to catch the person that is it as they race around the circle to get back to the "goose's" spot.

**Stop! Go! Fast! Slow!**
Give children actions to do (running, walking, jumping, crawling, dancing etc.) then give them instructions to "Stop!" and "Go!" and go "Fast" and "Slow".

**Musical Statues**
Play music and students freeze when the music stops.

## 3-6 years

### Hot and Cold
Hide an object and the children need to find it using your clues of calling out "hot" if they are close, "cold" if they are far away and "warm" if they are getting closer to the object.

### What's the Time Mr. Wolf?
Someone is Mr. Wolf and stands up one end, all the children stand down the other end. The children call out "What's the time Mr. Wolf?" Mr. Wolf calls out an o'clock time and the children take that many steps. As the children get closer Mr. Wolf calls out "Dinner time" chasing the children back to the start whilst trying to tag one of them. That person then becomes the next wolf.

### Balloon Up
Using a balloon children need to make sure that it stays in the air and doesn't land on the ground. They can keep it up with any of their body parts. You could also role play that it will be eaten by crocodiles or popped by hot lava if it touches the ground.

### Pizza Massage
Students sit in a circle all facing one direction so they can touch the student in front's back. Then, following the teacher's instructions, they will give them a pizza massage. Firstly, roll out the dough (roll fists over their back). Secondly, spread out the tomato paste (rub hands on their back). Next, cut up the ham, pineapple, salami, etc. (chop with the side of your hand). Then grate the cheese (use fingers to scratch) and sprinkle each ingredient on (use fingertips to sprinkle). Finally, warm up the pizza in the oven (rub their back fast), cut the pizza into 8 slices (slice with side of hand) and eat the pizza (grab at their back).

### Corners
Designate different corners or parts of the room as something they have been learning such as colours, shapes, numbers or letters. Children need to choose one and move to the area. You can then call or draw from a hat one of the corners and anyone standing in that corner needs to sit down.

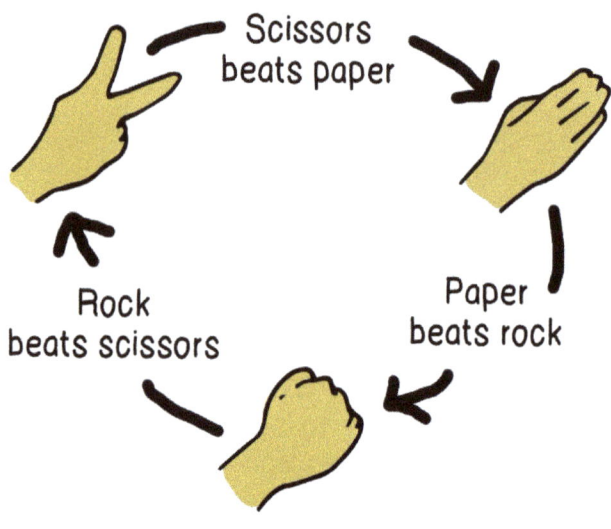

### Scissors, Paper, Rock
Teach the children the rules of this favourite hand game and how scissors beats paper, paper beats rock and rock beats scissors then get them to play with a partner.

## Mr Squiggle

Child draws a squiggle on the board and the teacher creates a picture out of it. Once the children understand how the game works then you can get the teacher to draw a squiggle on the board and a child can create a picture from the squiggle. You will need to model this game well at the start for it to be successful.

## Poison Letter

A caller chooses two letters to be the "poison letters". The caller is down one end and has their back to the children. They call out random letters and the children take a step for each letter that is in their name. They can take 2 steps if it is the first letter of their name. If they take a step when the poison letter is called out then they must go back to the beginning. The first to touch the callers back is the winner and becomes the next caller.

# NOTES

# NOTES

Time spent outdoor is a necessity for young children. It is a time when they can best practise their big movements or gross motor and physical skills to run, jump, skip, climb, throw, kick and swing.

Playing outdoors has many health benefits such as improving long distance vision, getting Vitamin D from sunlight, reducing stress and increasing their attention span.

Outdoor play helps them interact with their environment and provides endless open-ended opportunities for children to create, imagine, play and interact with their peers.

It is recommended that children play outside at least 3 times throughout the day. Around 30 minutes of adult-led activities along with at least an hour (preferably more) of unstructured play is the recommendation for young children.

**Open-ended activities**
Open-ended play is when children are free to imagine, create and play any way they like without set rules or limitations. Open-ended materials such as sand, water, clay, boxes, tyres, loose parts, blocks, sticks, rocks, material and paint have multiple uses and possibilities and allow children to create as they please.

These can be incorporated inside the classroom as well but there are many opportunities to implement this when setting up outdoor activities for the children.

# Outdoor Activities

"You can steer yourself any direction you choose."

**Dr. Suess**

Teacher for a Day

# 🚲 OUTDOOR ACTIVITY SET UP

This task can often get over looked and many times the same set up happens day after day. Keep things fresh for the children by creating interesting areas that vary from day to day. This will keep them more stimulated, active and engaged in their play.

**Sandpit**
Buckets and spades are fine in the sandpit but change it up sometimes by using less conventional materials and watch their imagination and the sandpit come to life!

**Add in-**

- small boxes, cartons and containers with spoons, ladles and utensils
- pots and pans, cutlery, teapots and tea cups
- large boxes, paper rolls and material
- chairs and table with dinner setting and play food
- sticks, rocks, pebbles and feathers
- trucks, workman hats, traffic signs
- small cars with cardboard ramps
- plastic or wooden blocks
- baby's baths and plastic dolls
- water trough with water play toys
- climbing frames, slides and tunnels

**Water Play**

What fun kids have with water, especially on a hot day. As much as we sometimes dread dealing with the mess and changes of clothes (Note- check and name clothes BEFORE you take them off!) there are lots of learning opportunities to be had and the children just love it!

Ideas for water play using a water trough and hose-

Add colour or glitter to the water.

Make leaf, paper, egg carton or plastic container boats then race them in a water trough.

Water trough with watering cans, funnels, cups and other water toys.

Add in plastic sea animals, or zoo or farm animals.

Put shells, rocks and plants and create a creek or river scene.

Explore sinking and floating with different objects.

Put on the sprinkler and let the children run through it.

Fill up baby baths and give them babies to wash and take care of.

Put the hose on the slide and create a waterslide for them to play on.

Put down a tarp and add some detergent and create a slip and slide.

Add in drink bottles and containers and explore volume by filling them up and asking which would hold more or less and test it.

Teacher for a Day

### Obstacle Course
Set up an obstacle course at the beginning of the day to provide a challenging activity for the children. Ideas on page 163.

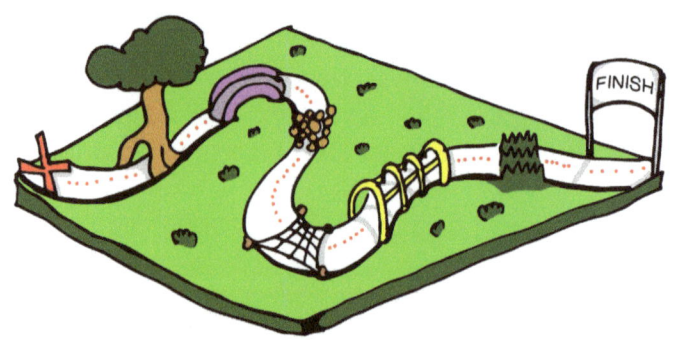

### Sport Time
Set up some structured activities for children to practise their skills.

- Put out balls with goals or hoops for them to score in
- Set up pins for tenpin bowling
- Put out racquet or bats with their accompanying balls
- Hula hoops and skipping ropes

### Bikes, Cars and Scooters
Bikes and cars are always popular. Ensure they are sharing with others and driving them safely. Try teaching the children how to push or pedal the vehicle.

### Fairy Garden
Set up a magical section of the yard to be the "Fairy Garden." Add in wind chimes, ribbon, dream catchers, bells, flowers, pebbles and glitter to add to the effect.

### Teddy Bears Picnic
Set up teddy bears and dolls on a blanket with some pillows, tea set, play food and some books.

Early Childhood Edition

### Bring Inside, Outside
Don't be afraid to step out of the "norm" of what should and shouldn't be. Set up a home corner inside the sandpit. Set up an office complete with keyboards, desk, chair and notepads under the fort. Put a book corner under the shade of the tree. Tie musical instruments to the trees, poles or fences.

### Cubbyhouse
Outdoor play is the perfect place to build a cubby. You may have a pop up tent or just make one out of sheets and blankets. Put in soft toys, books or dress ups to encourage imaginative play.

### Blocks
Set up different types of blocks each day in different areas of the yard to keep it novel. Add in cars, stuffed animals, plastic animals or figurines.

### Art and Craft
Give some creative options outside. Some simple ideas that don't need much assistance are-

- a drawing table could have crayons, pencils, textas, stencils or stamps
- painting with water paint palettes or water colours
- put up some spray painting (water paint in spray bottles) with newspaper pegged to the fence
- free collage with tape, glue, collaging material, boxes, container and paper

OUTDOOR ACTIVITIES

Teacher for a Day

# 🪂 PARACHUTE GAMES

Parachute games are great for building social interaction, listening skills, coordination and rhythm, turn taking and helps strengthen their torso. If you don't have a parachute you can always improvise with a large sheet or blanket.

**Waves**
Get children to coordinate their movements to make small, medium and large waves. Roleplay that you are sailing on the sea and the waves are getting bigger then smaller.

**Dome**
On the count of three get everyone to lift the parachute over their heads then crouch to the ground pulling the chute down, creating a dome over the group.

**Popcorn**
Place balls onto the parachute and shake them to make the "popcorn" pop. Sing "Popcorn in the frying pan, sizzling hot. Popcorn in the frying pan (jump up and shake the parachute vigorously) pop, pop, pop!

**Poisonous Snake**
Put three or four skipping ropes into the middle of the parachute and shake the parachute around to keep the snakes from biting/touching you.

*Early Childhood Edition*

**Parachute Tiggy**
Have the parachute lifted over head then call out a child's name to run, hop, skip, crawl to the other side before the parachute falls down and tags them.

**Rolling Ball**
Put a ball in the middle of the parachute and get children to control the ball to ensure it doesn't roll off.

**Name Change**
Call out two different children and they need to run underneath the parachute to swap places with the other person.

**Bouncy Balls**
Have one or two children under the parachute trying to hit the balls off. The rest of the group needs to try and keep them on.

# NOTES

# NOTES

Sustainability, conservation and the environment is an important subject to teach young children so that they can become responsible humans ready to make positive changes in the world.

We can do this by teaching them about wastage, recycling, pollution, caring for our environment and what will happen if we don't take care of our planet. Help educate them to become aware of the little changes we can make to help protect our Earth.

# Sustainability

"The greatest threat to our planet is the belief that someone else will save it."

**Robert Swan**

## Be Water Wise

Teach the children that it is important to conserve or not waste water. We don't have endless water and in times of drought (when it doesn't rain for long periods of time) we need to be especially careful with how we use our water.

*Ways to do this*

Discuss where you find water from all the different water sources e.g. taps, showers, baths, sinks, water tanks, ocean, river, lake, waterfall etc.

Explain how we need clean water to drink as our bodies are made up of water. Demonstrate how salt water from the ocean cannot be used for drinking water and experiment what happens to plants if we feed them salty water.

Nominate students to be Water Police and they need to make sure people are turning taps off in the bathroom when they are washing their hands or having a drink at the water fountain. They also need to look out for dripping taps as every drop counts!

Teach them to water the plants with left over water from their cups rather than tipping it down the drain or when doing water play that we do it on the grass not concrete so it can help the grass to grow.

*Early Childhood Edition*

# WASTE WARRIORS

Children need to understand what waste and litter is, how it can negatively impact our world and what we can do to fix it. The mantra of 'Reduce, Reuse and Recycle' is a great way to teach children ways to help save our environment.

## Litterbug

Educate the children on what happens if we litter (drop rubbish). Explain how it makes places look dirty and can attract rodents and cockroaches to the area. It is also dangerous for animals as sometimes they think the rubbish is food or get tangled up in it and this can make them very sick or even die.

Get children to go on a walk and pick up any rubbish they find. You could then sort the rubbish, discuss what it is, can it be recycled, could it harm the wildlife and why it is important that we put it in the bin.

There are some great books and online resources to extend on this.
For example, Litterbug Doug and Michael Recycle by Ellie Bethel.

## Reduce

*Reducing waste is when you try and produce less rubbish for landfill.* We can do this by making some better choices with what we buy and how we use things. Although young children aren't responsible for how much waste they produce, we can educate them and in turn they can influence others to make smarter choices.

Explain ways we can reduce our rubbish, such as saying "No" to plastic bags and taking reusable shopping bags into the shops instead. Encourage children to collect plastic bags in the home to recycle at the supermarket.

When storing our food, we can buy washable sandwich bags and glass or plastic containers to create a waste-free, "naked" lunchbox.

We can say "No" to throwaway water bottles and always take your own water bottle with you instead.

Be mindful of how much toilet paper you use when you go to the toilet. When drawing, try and use all the paper and even both sides so you don't waste as much. Little things can make a huge difference in this world and save money too!

**Reuse**

*Reusing rubbish is when we find another purpose for our waste.* This is common practise in early childhood by reusing rubbish to create art and craft projects.

Try and get the children to come up with new ways to reuse rubbish. For example a glass jar can become a pencil holder, an egg carton can be used to sort rocks or treasures, old birthday cards or wrapping paper can be cut up and reused for collage, plastic spoons can be repurposed to create a light shade etc.

**Recycle**

*Recycling is when rubbish is turned into a new product.* Explain that only certain types of rubbish can be recycled. We can recycle paper, cardboard, hard plastic, metal and glass.

Always lead by example. For classroom activities, make sure to buy and use paper from recycled sources, and show the children the difference between recycled and brand-new paper. Show them how to look for fruit tubs and muesli bars etc. from the supermarket that are in recycled packaging by looking for the recycled symbol.

Create recycling bins and get the children to sort different types of rubbish into the right bin. Explain the rules of recycling such as needing to remove the lids of bottle and jars before placing them in the bin, don't put recyclables in plastic bags or they will be sent to landfill, only glass jars and containers are suitable for glass recycling, soft plastics like straws, packaging and bags can't be recycled nor can hard plastic toys etc. Every bit counts, so saving a couple of items from landfill each week will help our planet out in a big way.

## Power Saver

Saving power not only helps save money but helps save the environment too. When we leave lights and fans on when we aren't in the room or when they aren't needed then it wastes electricity which is harmful for the environment. Energy Plants where we get our power from produce lots of pollution that goes into the sky. Although we don't see it, it can affect the air we breathe and can make people unwell. Discuss different ways we can get electricity- solar, wind, water etc. Have you seen any of these methods in real life? What happens with solar power if it is a cloudy, rainy day? Or wind power if it is not windy? You could create a model of a Wind Turbine or rivers flowing using recycled food packaging and art materials.

## Walk, Don't Drive

Every time we use the car we are sending pollution into the air. To reduce this we can choose to walk, ride a bike, bus, train or car share to get to where we need to go.

Ask the children if they can think of somewhere they usually drive but could possibly walk or ride to. Does their family like to go for bike rides? Have you caught the bus or train to get somewhere?

# NOTES

# NOTES

## Special Mention

I would firstly like to make a special mention to my illustrator and designer, Emmanuel Sambayan. Without his creative vision all my books would not be the appealing, easy-to-read resources that they are. Thanks a million! I couldn't have done it without you.

A second mention goes to Jodie and Jo for their amazing efforts in editing this book. It was a HUGE job and I am grateful for your keen attention to detail and input. You gals are legends.

The next mention goes to Linda, for introducing me to the world of Early Childhood Education and igniting my passion for teaching. For this, I will always be grateful.

Finally, I want to mention my mum, Kath. I am so proud of her dedication and persistence towards becoming an Early Childhood Educator. It was a long slog, but you got there. It just goes to show you are never too old to be learning new things and working towards a goal. You are an inspiration!

www.ingramcontent.com/pod-product-compliance
Lightning Source LLC
Chambersburg PA
CBHW040950020526
44118CB00045B/2829